Paul Harris was born in 1966. At the age of 34, after many years of spiritual enquiry and in search of a path and a teacher, Paul eventually found the House of Inner Tranquillity and met the Centre's co-founder Alan James. He ordained as a monk under Alan's guidance at The Monastery of Absolute Harmony in Bradford on Avon. In 2006, having completed his training, Paul was asked by Alan to succeed him as teacher and Spiritual Director of the Aukana Trust.

In addition to the meditation centre, the Trust also supports two monasteries for monks and nuns respectively. The Trust, therefore, is able to provide a comprehensive course of training for both lay students and full-time monastic recluses.

Paul disrobed in 2010 and continues to teach the path to enlightenment as well as directing the development of the monasteries and meditation centre.

Postcards From Beyond
by Paul Harris

AUKANA
BRADFORD ON AVON

"We shall not cease from exploration
And the end of all our exploring
Will be to arrive where we started
And know the place for the first time."

T. S. Eliot, *Four Quartets*

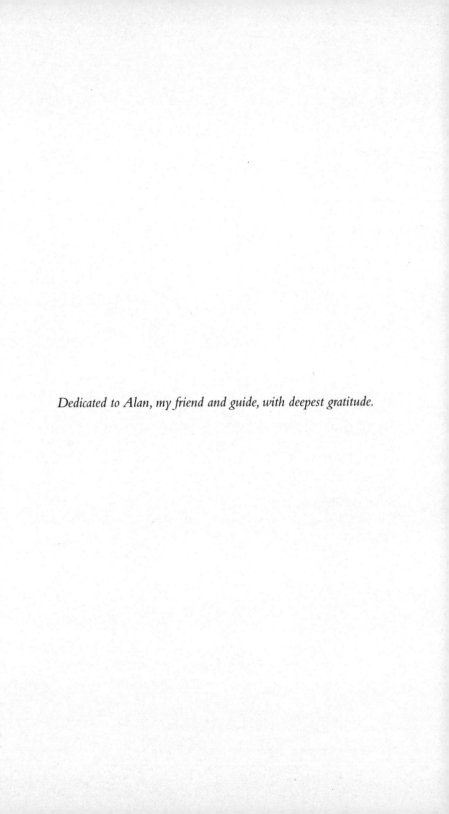

Dedicated to Alan, my friend and guide, with deepest gratitude.

First published 2014

Aukana Trust
9 Masons Lane
Bradford on Avon
Wiltshire
BA15 1QN
England

e-mail: info@aukana.org.uk
web:aukana.org.uk
Telephone: (01225) 866821, International: +44 1225 866821

The Aukana Trust is a registered charity (No 326938)

Typeset in Bembo 11/13.5
Printed in Great Britain by Biddles, King's Lynn, Norfolk

Cover design by Chris Harrison
web: harrison-agency.com

Acknowledgements
Quotes from the Pali Canon have been taken from translations by the
Pali Text Society.

A catalogue record for this book is available from the British Library

ISBN 978-0-9930054-0-4

Contents

Introduction xv

Life is Perfect As It Is 1

A Twenty-First Century Buddha 7

Sorrow is a Guru 13

The Art of Navigation 21

Harmlessness 29

Whatever Next!? 35

Holy Smoke 41

Letting the World Go Free 47

How Meditation Brings You to Your Senses 53

Solitude 59

Learning to Breathe 65

Making Friends with Your Demons 73

Dealing with the Dreamy Mind 81

Intent 87

Uses and Abuses of Mental Energy 93

Retrospection 99

Being Human 107

Cosmic Joke 115

The Building Blocks of Experience 121

Beyond Time and Space 127

What is Consciousness? 133

A Glimpse of the Beyond 141

Knowledge 151

Love 157

Dhamma Talks

    Trial and Error 167

    Feelings 173

    What Changes After Enlightenment? 179

Appendices

    I – Condition-Dependent Origination 187

    II – The Five Aggregates 189

Glossary of Pali Terms 195

Introduction

On the wall of my teacher's office hangs an ornate Thai Buddhist ceremonial fan, traditionally used by monks when they are teaching. The *Dhamma* teacher symbolically holds the fan to mask his face as he talks as a way of indicating that the teaching is being given free from any bias due to conceit, desire for acclaim or any other kind of personal advantage. It is done simply for the benefit of the listener.

As a meditation teacher writing my first book, I found myself confronted with many issues concerning quite how to put across this most extraordinary teaching. For instance, how much personal detail should there be in it? Was it profane to attempt to convey such deeply profound principles using personal anecdotes and humour? On the other hand, was it possible to give an authentic account of the Buddha's teaching without any of the author's individual character seeping through? I concluded that it was not.

Gaining insight into the Buddhist principle of non-self, does not equate to undergoing a charisma bypass. If anything, following this way you actually end up far more able to be yourself than you were before you started. My wish was to express something of what it *feels* like to enter wholeheartedly into a meditative training such as the Noble Eightfold Path and to do so in an entertaining way that might help to hold the reader's interest. Most importantly, I wanted to give expression to the fundamental truth that the goal of the Buddha's training, the cessation of suffering, is entirely real and attainable.

My experience of going through the *vipassanā* training is that it is far more intimate, messy and emotional than a purely academic rendering of it would, perhaps, depict. I fully appreciate, however, the need to be properly respectful, serious and accurate in conveying the Buddha's teaching. I have endeavoured, therefore, to balance the more emotive aspects of the training with a clear portrayal of the analytical precision and even-mindedness that is also developed.

Embarking upon the process of writing, I soon discovered how impossible it is to express adequately how *Buddha-Dhamma* is so completely flawless, logically consistent and powerfully effective. After all these years, I still feel a sense of awe whenever I contemplate how all the various strands of this teaching relate to one another and come together to create such a perfect whole. Real understanding of how all the pieces of the jigsaw fit together, however, can only come through undertaking the training and discovering it directly for oneself. All any book on Buddhism can do is offer a representative sample of what it is really all about. I have contented myself, therefore, with merely presenting a cross-section of the various layers of the training. In no way should the contents of this book be taken to embody the complete teaching.

A note on style. I think it was Albert Einstein who said that it was important that everything was made as simple as possible, but not any simpler. The Buddha's teaching is, in essence, very straightforward. In the telling, however, it does become more complicated. For simplicity's sake, I have decided to keep technical

Buddhist terms to a bare minimum. I have, however, retained the use of some Pali words like, for example, *dukkha*, *nibbāna* and *vipassanā*. This is partly because they are in such common usage in Buddhist circles, but also because the words often carry subtle gradations of meaning above and beyond anything their nearest and most suitable English counterparts convey. The meanings of Pali words are given when they first appear and a small glossary is included at the end of the book for those words that are used more regularly.

You will notice that I have kept the chapters quite short. My idea was for the book to be a series of reflections that would give meditation students food for thought and help stimulate the desire for real practice, but in a concise way. With our busy modern lifestyles not everyone has lots of free time that they can devote to reading. My intention was that each chapter would be a self-contained unit but that there would also be a natural and logical progression to their ordering. Each chapter can, there-fore, either be read in sequence or separately dipped into as each reader prefers.

★ ★ ★

I am not a writer by trade and communicating some pretty hefty ideas in a way that engages readers of all levels of interest has proved to be somewhat challenging. If I have come even vaguely close to achieving my aim then it could not have been without the generous help of others. I am very grateful to Alan James for looking over the manuscript and offering such cogent positive criticism. I would especially like to thank Keith Richardson who patiently worked through the entire book offering suggestions for tweaks to the punctuation and grammar. Thanks too to Brother Nigel, Sister Sara and Anda Lutkevics for their patience and support during what became a rather drawn-out process.

Finally I would like to thank all the students at the House of Inner Tranquillity who have devoted themselves so wholeheartedly to the training and for helping to make our *Saṅgha* the vibrant, friendly and steadfast community that it is.

Paul Harris
The House of Inner Tranquillity
Summer, 2014

Life is Perfect As It Is

You gently close the gate behind you and set out along the little track that winds round the crest of the hill. The path is lined on either side by a multitude of long grasses and colourful wild flowers, and you walk beneath an archway made of the over-hanging branches of a blossoming blackthorn tree. The mind is quiet and serene, and the body feels light and relaxed. There are no problems, no life issues crowd the mind and there are no riddles to be solved. Everything is perfect, just as it is.

The world is very beautiful this morning. Last night's rain has cleaned the air and the whole panorama appears crisp, clear and bright. Everything sparkles in the early morning light. Gazing out across to the forests on the other side of the valley, you notice the beautiful vivid green colour that spring growth has given to the leaves and marvel at the play of shadow and light on the treetops. In the valley below a train clatters past, you see a narrow-boat lazily chugging its way along the canal and joggers on the towpath are chatting to one another as they run.

Such activities in no way disturb the mind or spoil the view. The hustle and bustle of life is neither accepted nor rejected, but simply enveloped in the infinite peace and stillness; just part and parcel of all that is. The mind is quiet at that moment precisely because of the lack of value judgement and comparison. All is right as it is. There is no resistance. There is no "should" or "should not."

The track leads you down the hill towards the little stone bridge that crosses the canal. In a hedgerow nearby blackbirds are singing sweetly and a jackdaw, sitting on a telegraph pole, lets out a throaty call, flaps its wings and takes smoothly to the air. The warmth of the sun touches the back of your neck and from nowhere a most delicate rapture arises, filling every fibre of your being with love and contentment.

★ ★ ★

Life is perfect as it is. It does not require any change to make it perfect; it is perfect right now. There is an awesome quietness within every experience. Even the most chaotic of situations are contained within a most profound stillness. In every experience, behind everything else, there is an exquisite silence; it makes no difference if it is during a meeting at work, being caught up in the rush hour traffic, sitting at home watching the television, during a bar-room brawl, being lost in a foreign city, making love or tending to a dying relative.

Life is inherently simple, self-explanatory and harmonious. What complicates matters and makes a sore trial of life is the psychological "white-noise" of forever wanting things to be different and wishing life to be different means never noticing the stillness that resides at the heart of it all. Perfection is what is left, whenever the white-noise of resistance is absent.

Change is inevitable, experiences come and go, but this perfect quietude remains. It is not a thing in itself. You cannot own it. It cannot be labelled or pigeon-holed or pointed to and it will not conform to any perception ascribed to it Even to express it as "stillness" or "silence" is to misconceive it. It is so subtle that to even look for it is to deny its existence. Despite this, however, it remains eminently discoverable and once you have truly apprehended it, you know that it is the only truly real thing there is and the existence of anything else is mere appearance at best.

To suggest that life is perfect is a very dangerous idea. The vast majority of people do not experience life as being perfect and would likely take exception to being told it was. The evidence of suffering is all around us. Whose lives have not been touched with the anguish of serious illness or bereavement? What about the wars and violence, the greed and corruption, the poverty, hunger and injustice; not to mention the earthquakes, tsunamis and other natural disasters? Outwardly there is so much evidence of life's apparent imperfection, how could it be said to be perfect?

The perception of life as being all wrong is also reflected inwardly. So much of the time it can feel as though there is an invisible barrier between oneself and the world, and a painful dislocation from the peace, happiness and success to which we aspire. Most of our time and energy, consequently, is spent in trying to bridge the perceived gap between how life appears and how we think it ought to be.

How deeply the human mind is conflicted! After so many thousands of years of intelligent existence our basic psychological condition has changed little. The many forms of neurosis to which human beings are prone still exist; states such as greed, hatred, confusion, fear, worry, loneliness and depression. Psychologically, we are mostly anywhere but contentedly enjoying life here and now. In place of stillness, we know only disquiet.

This is not to say that life cannot provide us with pleasure and relative happiness; it most certainly can. With varying degrees of success we all manipulate life to give us an approximation of what we really want. We have produced a multitude of belief systems and philosophies to explain our condition and which offer us solace, hope and a way of managing our doubts and uncertainties. We have fashioned countless ways to entertain and distract ourselves via the arts, sport, technology and the like. It is true that we are clever, cultured and creative. No matter, however, what we design and produce, no matter how much we consume, whenever we stop, inevitably, we are confronted with restlessness, fear and dissatisfaction. The human condition is one of constant motion; forever searching, finding, possessing and losing, over and over again.

Yet there is something beyond the ceaseless flow of time, space and activity. There is a deep, profound stillness that persists amidst the ever changing flux of conscious experience, and when it is discovered, you know intuitively that it is what everyone is really looking for. It is, if you will, the universal goal of peace and contentment to which each of us aspires. It is always present and its discovery is never denied us, but it is subtle and hard to see. This means it is most often just simply ignored, covered over by the incessant and slavish need to make life different than it is.

There are, however, rare occasions when life affords us a tantalising glimpse of the very perfection we seek. Perhaps we are absorbed in a beautiful piece of music or something completely unexpected happens and at such times there is a temporary suspension of our habitual thought processes and neurotic preoccupations. A sense of timelessness becomes apparent and with it a comprehension of how simple life can be and of how effortlessly everything happens. What was previously overlooked as being too ordinary and familiar is now seen in a new, mysterious and beautiful light. It feels as though everything is in its rightful place and there is a deep sense of familiarity, as if being reunited with a long-forgotten friend.

Such experiences cannot last. Once over, many simply return to their usual, habitual preoccupations and the event is not regarded as significant and easily forgotten. For others, the accompanying feelings of benevolence, love and a subtle yet glorious rapture, leave a deep impression and are so intense that they can change the entire course of a person's life, for the apparent loss of that profound connection creates a deep yearning to rediscover it.

★ ★ ★

Two and a half thousand years ago, an Indian sage by the name of Siddartha Gotama realised this true stillness that lies at the heart of life. He discovered it through the spontaneous ending of all psychological becoming and searching. He abandoned all passionate desire for life to be different and instead, remaining mindful, self possessed and free from all bias, he gave his un-qualified attention to observing life as it occurred in real time, moment by moment and simply watched. And what did he find? Life, he discovered, is perfect as it is.

Henceforth, Gotama became known as the Buddha, which means "Awakened One." He realised that it is through not un-derstanding how life works that creates all the resistance that causes suffering. With his enlightenment, the murk of ignorance had been dispelled and all suffering had ceased for him and could never now return. He was finally at peace. He called this perfect stillness *nibbāna* and maintained that it is the highest happiness to which anyone can aspire.

The Buddha never claimed to be the first or only person to have discovered *nibbāna*. What differentiates Gotama from others was his ability to create an effective teaching, whereby anyone can, with proper application, arrive at that same realisation. He likened *nibbāna* to an ancient city and suggested that what he had done was to rediscover the lost path that led to it. He knew that *nibbāna* is what all beings are trying so hard to find and out of compassion for suffering humanity he showed the way to discover it.

Time, dedication and much in the way of personal development is required to eradicate that perpetual white-noise of dissatisfaction, for its roots run ever so deep. Once, however, our inner demons have been overcome, once we are truly no longer craving for life to be different than it is and have given up all attachment to the things of the world, then there is nothing to prevent the total comprehension of the exquisite peace and perfection of *nibbāna*.

A Twenty-First Century Buddha

During the seventeenth and eighteenth centuries there was a dramatic flowering of human thought that became known as the Age of Reason. The driving force behind this philosophical revolution was the desire for human affairs to be guided by rationality rather than by faith, superstition or revelation. Gradually, the conviction grew that human reason alone had the power to change society and could liberate the individual from the shackles of custom, blind belief and arbitrary authority. This principle was backed up by a world view increasingly authenticated by science rather than by religion.

This credo, so influential in advancing civilisation and broadening our horizons for over three hundred years, is still very much at the heart of our twenty-first century world. Society appears to be increasingly secular these days, with religious views and traditional spiritual values seemingly on the back-foot; at least for the time being.

Our culture greatly values scientific rigor, objective proof, logical thought and rational argument and considers blind belief, superstition and unquestioning subjugation to the authority of others, as outdated and dangerous. People increasingly, are not accepting things as being true just because someone in a powerful position tells them it is so. The modern outlook demands, not unjustifiably, evidence of the existence of something before trust is placed in it. Scepticism and doubt are fashionable and there is a burden placed upon all spiritual traditions to substantiate the beliefs they uphold.

The Buddha lived in India five hundred years before the Romans conquered Britain, a very different age. Could such an ancient teaching have any relevance in today's world, with such firebrand scepticism so firmly rooted in our culture?

Reading the Buddha's discourses in the Pali Canon we discover that Gotama held a moderate and progressive attitude regarding questions of belief and free inquiry. Spiritual discourse has always been an indelible part of the Indian culture and wandering mendicant monks would always find an audience in the villages and towns that was eager to listen to what they had to say.

Once, on one of his regular walking tours, Gotama stopped off at the village of Kesaputta. The people of Kesaputta, the Kalamas, found that the various teachers who visited all had widely differing views and would expound their own ideas as being the truth and would disparage and condemn the views of others. In the end the Kalamas became confused and doubtful, not knowing whom to believe.

The advice the Buddha gave the villagers has since become famous as a compelling argument against the diktats of dogmatism and blind belief in preference for direct, personal investigation. He counselled them against accepting an idea as being true simply on the basis that it was a traditionally held belief or because other peoples' testimonies sounded plausible. Neither should they be taken in by the mere skill of the orator. Just because a particular declaration seemed reasonable, logical or happened to meet with their approval did not mean that it was right. Nor should they accept an assertion simply out of respect for the person who held it, no matter how revered he or she may be.

Care must be taken with this message. The Buddha was not dismissing all doctrine, faith or spiritual guidance out of hand. He was not inviting the Kalamas to accept or reject whatever they like according to their whim. Gotama told them that the only acceptable criteria to judge a particular spiritual way must come from putting its principles into practice and finding out directly for themselves.

It is direct personal experience alone that will properly inform us as to whether something is right or wrong, true or false, and whether it reduces and eliminates suffering or not. Mindful investigation of life and the ability to wisely reflect on our experience are integral characteristics of the Buddha's teaching and he insisted that everything he taught was personally discoverable through one's own efforts.

To undertake such an investigation without knowing what the result will be requires faith. Faith is a positive human quality. To have faith is to have confidence, which is not at all the same thing as blind belief. Without faith we would never accomplish anything. You would not expect a scientist standing before his equipment to say: "I will not perform this experiment until I have a guarantee that it will have a successful outcome." The scientist performs his experiment with uncertainty as to the outcome, but with the confidence that, whatever the result, he will be more knowledgeable as a consequence.

By the same token, adopting a set of religious beliefs with no way of verifying their authenticity for oneself is a total abdication of personal responsibility. You have to be willing to place your beliefs at risk through undertaking a proper examination of life. In just the same way as with the scientist, you begin from a position of uncertainty as to the outcome, but with the confidence that you will be wiser for it; even if what you find disproves the beliefs that you had previously held.

To explain another way, consider the sceptic's notion that you often come across: "I'll believe it when I've seen it."

This idea is a complete nonsense, isn't it? If you have seen it then you no longer need to believe it. All beliefs are attempts to escape from the uncertainty of not knowing. You believe precisely because you do not know. Once you have understood, belief becomes entirely superfluous. To understand, however, you must be free to investigate and to investigate freely you must first be willing to accept that you do not know. Not knowing is to remain in and investigate from a position of uncertainty. And that requires faith.

Faith and investigation are partners not enemies. They are both positive and necessary functions of the human psyche and having the two working in harmony is essential to a person's well-being and enjoyable participation in life.

Religion and science are united in the sense that they are both expressions of the same fundamental human desire to find "the truth that sets us free." The Buddha's core teaching is that complete freedom from suffering is potentially available to anyone and he provides us with the tools with which to investigate life and discover that freedom for ourselves.

To do this, however, we must begin from a position of uncertainty and openness, with our current view structures, whether secular or religious, held lightly in our hands. It is also imperative to use the tools wisely and this requires us to place our faith in the guidance of a teacher and to undertake spiritual practices as instructed. Only then is it possible to properly ascertain the effectiveness of what the Buddha taught.

Gotama advised his students to test the training by entering into it under the guidance of a capable teacher. He said that, if after practising properly for an appropriate length of time, they found that suffering did not diminish and wisdom did not grow, then they were to leave that teacher and go off and find another; even if he was the most highly revered teacher in the world. If, however, they found that their suffering did diminish and wisdom did grow, then they were never to leave that teacher's side; even if he drove them off with a stick.

From the evidence of his message to the Kalamas, we can see that the Buddha's teaching is perfectly in harmony with our pragmatic, twenty-first century outlook and actually goes much further than the ideas and values introduced during the Age of Reason. Buddha-Dhamma is flexible, reasonable, rational and intelligent. It encourages an open-minded attitude, along with a spirit of enquiry, balanced with an equal amount of faith and the overarching desire to find out the truth for oneself.

Sorrow is a Guru

All life is non-dual. In reality there are no separate things that exist distinct and independently from one another. Life comes all of a piece. Given that there are no things, this means that there is nothing that is born and nothing that is subject to change, decay and death. Hence there is no suffering. Just this is perfection, this is peace. The comprehensive realisation of non-duality is *nibbāna*. It is the permanent freedom and happiness that lies beyond the endless tumult of dualistic existence.

To the enlightened mind, the conventional reality that most people take for granted as being absolutely real, is understood to be illusory. The beings, objects, locations and events that appear to exist in a solid and reliable state, do so only because of a deep existential ignorance or blindness *(avijjā)*. Even time, space, matter and consciousness share this same hallucinatory quality.

The apparent existence of any one thing depends upon an infinite number of other conditions being present. Remove or change just one of these and in that instant that "thing" ceases to be. You cannot have an object separate from the conditions that go to make it up. Delimit reality into separate entities and in that moment the truth of non-duality is obscured. The objects thus created are deeply unsatisfactory, subject as they are to change, decay and death.

In Buddhism dualistic existence is called *saṃsāra*. In contra-distinction to *nibbāna*, it is not happy, peaceful or free. This is because conditions are always changing which make life funda-mentally unstable and unreliable. To identify with and rely on anything within dualistic existence for one's happiness therefore guarantees suffering.

The enlightened mind sees and understands both *nibbāna* and *saṃsāra*. The enlightened mind, therefore, does not make the mistake of identifying with and developing attachments towards anything in the dualistic world. Its appearance is clearly com-prehended as being deceptive and empty of any intrinsic reality. The enlightened mind does not hanker and crave for life to be different and is, therefore, tranquil.

The unenlightened mind, on the other hand, neither sees nor understands *nibbāna* or *saṃsāra*. Blinded by ignorance, the unen-lightened mind fundamentally misperceives dualistic existence. It is seen and believed to be intrinsically real, ongoing, stable and reliable. This hallucination is clung to regardless of the fact that the things of the world always let us down. Whenever the unenlightened mind is confronted by the real facts of life, such as loss or change, it suffers. Ignoring these self-evident facts, it instead responds with the passionate desire for life to be different. Believing that life should be different, it clings to that notion and attempts to make it so. This generates endless suffering, because whatever new pattern is created, it will still have the same inher-ent nature to change, decay and die. As a friend of mine once quipped, "If life was a stick of rock, *dukkha* (suffering) would be the word running through it."

Rarely does the unenlightened mind question the validity of these first assumptions and consequent misperceptions. Rarely

does the unenlightened mind look up from its endless preoccupations and self-absorption to look at *saṃsāra* directly and see
it for what it is.

A rare occurrence it may be, but this is not to suggest that it
never happens. The Tibetans have a saying that sorrow is a guru,
because it teaches us the need to live a spiritual life. It is the
direct personal experience of the repeating patterns of craving
and suffering that eventually cause us to reflect wisely and begin
asking fundamental questions about the nature of life. This was
certainly the case with Gotama. He renounced his cosseted life
of royal privilege and undertook the spiritual search as a penniless wanderer only after having been confronted with the realities
of disease, old age and death.

The question that inevitably arises is how. How do you face up
to reality, where do you look and what is it exactly that you are
looking for? Finding *nibbāna* is not at all easy. It is not located
anywhere, it cannot be described, thought about or perceived
by the senses. It lies altogether beyond time, space, matter, and
consciousness. In addition, it is so subtle and intimate, that the
very act of looking for it, obscures it.

Yet, for all of that, people do find it. Moreover, they maintain
that when you do finally realise what it is, it is then as obvious as
a gooseberry sitting in the palm of your hand. This is an important point to bear in mind. Although when we try to describe
enlightenment it may appear to be a rather complex and baffling
conundrum, the true comprehension of it, however, is utterly
simple and self-explanatory.

Gotama undertook the search for *nibbāna* out of compassion for
all beings. When he did realise the truth, it was entirely through
his own efforts and without any help from anyone else. That he
actually found the needle in the haystack without any guidance
is awesome enough, but he was able to accomplish even more.

Despite the fact that enlightenment is a non-conceptual understanding, he was, nonetheless, able to fashion and communicate a complete and effective teaching. Through this anyone can, with the requisite endeavour, come to realise exactly what he had realised. We call what he taught *buddha-dhamma* and the precision, economy, logic and, above all, effectiveness of his exposition make for a teaching of flawless beauty. It is truly a masterpiece. The Buddha's great contribution to humanity was to provide us with the "how."

★ ★ ★

The Buddha encapsulated his realisation very precisely in what he called the Four Noble Truths. The first is that life, as seen from the dualistic standpoint, really is suffering. The second is that craving born of ignorance is the cause of suffering. The third truth is that *nibbāna* is real and it is entirely possible for anyone to realise the complete cessation of suffering. Finally, the fourth truth confirms that there is a way to achieve this, the Noble Eightfold Path. This consists of right view, right thought, right action, right speech, right livelihood, right effort, right mindfulness and right concentration.

From the very outset it is critically important to understand that the Buddha's teaching is not designed to produce a future result. Although, paradoxically, we must also appreciate that realising enlightenment will take time.

To explain, non-duality is real now, even as you read these words. It is not something that needs to be created. You cannot make *nibbāna* happen anymore than you can make the sun shine, because it always is. When the sun is obscured by cloud we say that the sun has not come out today, but actually we know that it is always there shining. In the same way, *nibbāna* is always right here, now but hidden behind a thick fog of ignorance, wrong

views, misperceptions and the myriad activities born of craving
and clinging attachment.

So, the student of *buddha-dhamma* is not trying to produce enlightenment. Rather, the task is to extinguish the fires of craving
and eliminate the smoke of ignorance, for these are the things
that obscure the radiant, eternal truth. To do this, however, we
need to develop our mental faculties and it is this process which
takes the time.

How does the path work? The fulcrum upon which the whole
training turns is mindfulness, along with clear comprehension.
Mindfulness is the choice-less awareness of whatever is present
in our experience right now. Clear comprehension is the understanding of what we are experiencing in the context of our
aspiration to realise *nibbāna*.

Mindfulness, the Buddha said, was the one way to overcome
suffering. Paying detailed and systematic attention to conscious
experience as it unfolds, allows us to learn directly about how
life really works. In the process, we undo all the wrong views
and misperceptions that create and perpetuate attachment to
the illusion of duality, and all the suffering that then ensues. In
Buddhism, we call this seeing into and comprehending reality,
insight-wisdom. It is wisdom that dissipates the fog of ignorance.

Mindfulness is the opposite of ignorance and can arise only in
the absence of craving. This means that sustained effort must also
be made in learning how consciously to restrain acts of craving
in body, speech and mind. Otherwise, the mind is forever caught
up in its neurotic preoccupations and displacement activities, and
continues to ignore reality. Living an ethical life and training the
mind to be quiet help to create a spacious, calm mind, which is
a vital prerequisite for developing insight.

So, for ease of exposition, we can condense the factors of the
Noble Eightfold Path into three trainings, those of *sīla* or ethical

conduct, *samādhi* or mental control, and *paññā* or wisdom. These three trainings are undertaken together. They are like the legs of a tripod in that each one simultaneously depends upon and helps to support the other two. Take up and develop one aspect of the training and, in doing so, you begin to develop it all.

To sum up, we suffer whenever we crave for life to be different than it is. The roots of all craving lie in a fundamental and profound misapprehension of life. To release ourselves from suffering we must cease to ignore the way life really is and instead pay exquisite mindful attention to reality as it unfolds moment by moment. In this way we produce the insight-wisdom that eventually destroys this ongoing fundamental delusion. The Buddha's teaching compassionately guides us in how to do this.

★ ★ ★

For some people the idea of non-duality might appear a bit far-fetched. After all, it is obvious that there are "things" isn't it? Or perhaps the descriptions that are offered appear too philosophical, too heady or seem to be a little too divorced from the realities of everyday life. Fortunately, with the Buddha's teaching, you are not being asked to blindly believe anything that you do not want to believe.

The real driving force behind true engagement with *buddha-dhamma* is the realisation of the all-encompassing nature of *dukkha*. The motivation to follow this way comes when you finally wisely reflect upon the fact that no matter how hard you try, no matter how many different options you employ or directions in life you take, the genuine lasting peace to which you aspire never actually materialises. You finally notice the recurring pattern, that notwithstanding your very real achievements in life, you are still haunted by a basic state of discontentedness. You reflect that you have tried as many worldly ways as you can think of to assuage that sense of dissatisfaction and that none of them have ultimately worked. Despite that constant endeavour, you are still subject to the same old fear, anxiety, pain and distress. You are still liable to disease, old age and death. You still lose the things you love, are united with things you do not love and cannot get the things you want. You find that you are still left with the same fundamental questions that have secretly always been troubling you, "Why am I suffering? When will I be truly happy? What is life for?"

It is a very humbling moment to realise that you do not know. Yet, to know that you do not know, that is where the true path to understanding begins.

The Art of Navigation

For thousands of years sailors have been able to cross the huge oceans successfully by measuring the position of celestial bodies such as the sun, the moon, planets and stars against the visible horizon, and are thus able to calculate their location and navigate their journey accurately. To have guiding principles, to have some fixed point from which to draw measurements, means that we are far less likely to go astray and can reach our chosen destination safely.

The Buddha's way to enlightenment begins with Right View and Right Thought as the first two steps. The choices we make in life, the direction we take and the kind of actions of body, speech and mind that we perform, are all informed and motivated by the kinds of views that we hold. We all have views about life. To make sense of the world, everyone needs guiding principles. Without creating such definitions, life remains an amorphous mass and is impossible to navigate at all. We would be well and truly lost.

One of the criticisms levelled at this modern, secular age, is that with the gradual replacement of religion with science as the primary influence on popular attitudes, we are in danger of

losing many of the core human values and guiding principles
that have helped to glue society together. In the news media we
regularly hear about people whose "moral compass" appears to
have gone haywire and it can appear as though society is filled
to the brim with greedy bankers, corrupt politicians, debauched
stars and boorish, disaffected youths.

Whilst there are unquestionably many critical ethical issues that
face modern society, is it really the case that we are being swept
away by a dismal tide of interminable moral decline? Isn't it the
case that, "It wasn't like that in my day," is heard in every generation looking, with something of a shudder, at the behaviour of
the next. The Buddha maintained that ignorance and craving are
the indispensable conditions necessary for anybody to be born
into our world and these core defilements are therefore already
firmly established in the personality of everyone. This being the
case, is it not inevitable that every generation will have its fair
share of trouble and lessons to learn?

Some argue that, in this era of globalization, we now need to
establish a set of universal values; a moral and ethical framework
upon which all are in agreement, irrespective of creed or culture.
Is that possible, however, given quite how complex and varied
human beings and their belief systems are? "Right" and "wrong"
are to be determined by whom? Could a liberal materialist and
a religious fundamentalist ever be expected to agree upon the
same definitions? It seems unlikely.

In Buddhism "wrong" is always defined by that which leads to
the production and increase in suffering for either oneself or
others or both. "Right" is always defined by that which leads to
the reduction and elimination of suffering for either oneself or
others or both. But these are not just theoretical notions of right
and wrong. As my teacher Alan has often said: "Buddhism isn't
something you just think about, it is something you do."

The point is that our understanding of right and wrong is informed directly from our own life experience of what genuinely leads to woe, sorrow and lamentation, and what genuinely leads to peace, happiness and fulfilment. So there is no forceful imposition of values on others in Buddhism; there can be no inquisition. The Buddha gives us the guiding principles and the tools we need to navigate our way, but we are all individually the captain of our own ship and personally responsible for our "moral compass." It is up to us.

The Buddha taught how life works using two distinct but interweaving philosophies. He taught a conventional or mundane wisdom relating to the everyday world showing us how to navigate our way around life. He also taught ultimate or supramundane wisdom. Sometimes referred to as his "higher teaching," it is this aspect of what he taught that leads to the complete elimination of craving, hatred and ignorance and to the direct realization of *nibbāna*, the beyond.

The relationship between these two teachings can be understood using an analogy that the Buddha employed. Gotama likened *saṃsāra* to a great expanse of water with two banks either side. The near shore represents ignorance with countless beings running to and fro, blindly trying to find their way out of suffering. The far shore represents the understanding of the way life really is, the hallmark of the enlightened mind. The Buddha likened his teaching to a raft that takes us from the near shore of ignorance to the far shore of understanding. The primary purpose of his teaching is enlightenment and that is the province of his higher teaching. The subsidiary purpose was to help ensure that we have as pleasant a voyage as possible and that is the purpose of his mundane teaching. Whether the crossing is rough or smooth is actually dependent on our own behaviour. Indeed, without moderating our behaviour it is impossible to complete the voyage.

The Buddha gave a simple five-point plan for ensuring relative happiness in life now and in the future. In Buddhism we call this the five points of Mundane Right View and they are "right" in the sense of accurately reflecting the rules of life and because they result in a reduction in suffering for those who adopt them and act in accordance with them. They are:

- Actions have results
- Generosity benefits the giver
- There are mother and father
- There are spontaneously arisen beings
- There are teachers who know about these things and who can show us the way

These five points suffuse and permeate the whole of the Buddha's teaching and they will be integral components in any discussion of life as seen from the Buddhist perspective, including the contents of this book. That being the case, we will limit ourselves to a brief overview of each:

"Actions have results"

The conditions we experience now are the fruits of our own previous actions. Selfish actions lead to the arising of painful feelings and unwanted perceptions now and in the future, while relatively unselfish, altruistic actions produce pleasant results both now and in the future.

This is *kamma* and its law cannot be broken. It is a fact of mundane experience in the same way that the law of gravity is. Just as what goes up must come down, so any action taken with a view of self must generate a result *(kamma-vipāka)* that is experienced by the doer.

"There is a result of giving"

This reinforces the principle of *kamma* with the added emphasis of presenting people with a simple method to find out whether the law of action and result is real. Generosity applies not just to money. Food, shelter, encouragement or generating loving thoughts are all forms of giving that produce positive results. Being generous also reduces self concern, lessens attachments and increases our faith in life, all of which are essential supports when it comes to practising the higher teaching.

"There are Mother and Father"

This view connects the two preceding points with the two that are to follow and is pivotal in helping us form a comprehensive view of how the world works.

Most of us, at times, will have had difficult relations with our parents, especially during the period of the adolescent rebellion. Viewed, however, in the wider context of the cyclical nature of existence and the workings of *kamma*, what becomes clear, is that it is our own past actions that have caused us to be born with these people as our parents. The early life conditioning fashioned by our upbringing, moreover, is an integral part of our journey from ignorance to understanding. The circumstances we are born into, therefore, are entirely right for us.

To maintain a grudge toward our parents about how we were raised is to misunderstand the workings of the world and will seriously impair our own development. Although we may disagree with their opinions or behaviour, they still deserve our respect. They have done so much for us in bearing the pain of bringing us into the world and making enormous sacrifices to give us a start in life.

Understanding the crucial link that our parents provide, treating them or their memory in an honourable way and developing an even-minded attitude towards our early-life conditioning, are all aspects of what this point of mundane wisdom means.

"There are spontaneously arisen beings"

Many people these days hold a belief that there is only one life and that the death of the physical body is annihilation, the absolute end of conscious experiencing. Although such a belief is often taken to be a key signifier of a modern, rational, post-religious outlook, the idea is actually as old as the hills.

In the discourses contained in the Pali Canon, the Buddha is often engaged in discussing the full spectrum of possible beliefs around what happens at death, including the one-life theory. The Buddha knew from his own experience that when someone dies from the human realm, they spontaneously reappear in another form of existence. Where a being reappears is dependent on their *kamma*, essentially how they lived their lives; how they acted in body, speech and mind.

The idea here is that we have all experienced countless lives before and will also continue to experience countless lives in the future.

"There are teachers who know about these things"

The five points of mundane right view are rounded off with a strong reminder that, as with everything in life, there are others with a greater knowledge and understanding than us, who are able and willing to guide us. Using the analogy of attempting to cross the sea of suffering on a raft, there are those who have already reached the far shore who can help others complete the journey. After all, if we already knew the way and did not need telling, we would already be there. An open, generous and humble attitude towards receiving spiritual guidance is crucial to successfully navigating one's way.

These five points of mundane right view were not arbitrarily plucked from thin air by the Buddha. He expounded them because they represent the most accurate reflection of the way the world works. Adopting these views opens up a radically different context for understanding life and our journey through it. Accepting that we are personally responsible for the circumstances that we find ourselves in puts us in control of our lives. Our destiny really is in our own hands. If you want to know what the future has in store for you, observe your behaviour now. If you wish to ensure a happy future, then you must take responsibility for the ethical quality of your behaviour. The more selfish the behaviour, the more painful life becomes, whereas the more relatively unselfish the behaviour, the more pleasant life becomes.

Establishing Mundane Right View is the essential first step in developing the threefold training in *sīla*, *samādhi* and *paññā*. The nature of the training is such that we need to be able to sit by ourselves quietly in order to look deeply into the heart of reality. To do this we need to be "comfortable in our own skin." We need to have a relatively healthy view of ourselves, our past, our future and the world around us. If we are caught up in an overly turbulent lifestyle or are at odds with the way life is, then this is just not possible.

This becomes even more crucial as we begin to delve into the Buddha's higher teaching, where our most basic assumptions and beliefs about life are brought under intense scrutiny and challenged through *vipassanā*, insight meditation.

Enlightenment, the discovery of the true nature of life, is freedom from the need to hold any beliefs whatsoever. Concluding his analogy of the raft, the Buddha said that upon reaching the far shore, the final act was to leave the raft and walk on without it. For there to be true freedom there can be no clinging, not even to the very teaching that brought you to the greatest understanding of all. In the end all views have the nature to divide, even "right" ones and wherever there is division, there is conflict and sorrow. The Buddha taught the way to enlightenment purely out of compassion for his fellow beings, it was the ultimate act of disinterested love; he, himself, wanted nothing from it. His teaching, he said, was for "crossing over, not retaining."

Harmlessness

Nibbāna is the understanding that transcends the endless play of opposites found in the relative world. It is complete freedom from all neurotic preoccupations about where you, I or anything else appears on the sliding scale between "right and wrong", "good and bad" or "acceptable and unacceptable." With the comprehension of non-duality, all ignorant craving for life to be different is expunged forever.

This means that the enlightened man or woman is free from having to live specifically by any ethical code. This is not to imply that they exist in some amoral vacuum, a law unto themselves. It is, rather, that their natural disposition is no longer being warped by greed, hatred and delusion. The enlightened man or woman performs no unwholesome action of body, speech or mind and they are no longer a cause of suffering in the world. Their actions are spontaneous, blameless and free, irrespective of how they may be perceived from the outside.

The journey of inner discovery, however, that eventually culminates with full enlightenment, does require that we live by an ethical code. We all come into this world with greed, hatred and delusion deeply rooted within us and, therefore, we all have the potential to be a harmful influence. To follow the meditative path successfully necessitates a gentle and compassionate outlook. How can we be mindful and investigate life with insight if we are at one and the same time cruelly abusing and exploiting it? We need to have an open, caring and guilt-free relationship with the world. Harming and cruelty are born of ignorance and selfishness, and consequently lead to an ever greater sense of separation and isolation – in stark contrast to the reality of non-duality.

An intrinsic part of the Buddhist way of life is to live by the Precepts. These are five guidelines that regulate one's personal behaviour and, as a result, help to ensure that we are as harmless as possible.

The five are:

I undertake the rule of training to refrain from...

...killing or harming living creatures
...taking that which is not given
...sexual misconduct
...wrong speech
...intoxication and mind-altering drink and drugs

All beings value their life and no-one wishes to experience pain. At the heart of it, keeping precepts is the endeavour to treat all living beings, including oneself, in exactly the same way that we ourselves would like to be treated.

The result of abiding by these injunctions is a guilt-free existence and a greater sense of being a part of a benevolent, friendly universe. There is less of a necessity to close off psychologically to protect ourselves from the rest of the world because we experience less in the way of external conflict and we have few causes for regret.

The training in ethics is natural and unforced. The precepts are not commandments as in "thou shalt not..." Rather they are tools for training, guidelines to be adhered to because someone sees the benefit to them personally in doing so.

In the last analysis we are all free to behave as we wish. We are free to pick up a trumpet and make as much of a racket as we want, but someone who takes the time and trouble to learn the rules of music and how to play the instrument properly can then use it to create something of great beauty.

Developing an ethical lifestyle is no different. When we look at the world around us with all its war, crime and economic catastrophe, we see a place in which people are struggling to learn the rules that govern life's ethical dimension. The intelligent student is therefore happy to forego their freedom to "do what thou wilt" whenever they feel like it. They have a far nobler vision of what true freedom is.

Just as when we learn anything, we are bound to make mistakes. No-one can keep all the precepts perfectly all the time. In fact as a teacher, it is quite telling when a meditator tries to give you the impression that they do. If you are genuine in attempting to keep the precepts as best you can, then an occasional lapse is not an issue. Breaking precepts does not make you a bad person anymore than hitting a bum-note on a trumpet does.

Of course, if people pay absolutely no heed to the results of their own blameworthy actions then they will end up in a hellish existence, both in this life and in lives to come. Even then, however, that does not make them intrinsically bad people, it is simply the workings of the impersonal law of *kamma*.

Whenever we perform an unwholesome action in body or speech, as a natural result we experience a painful feeling and a sense of guilty dread or regret. It is not in any way personal, it is the same for everyone.

What many people do is misread the guilty feeling and, taking it personally, react by justifying or blaming themselves and others. If, rather than trying to avoid these inevitable resultants, you are willing to be mindful of them and to acknowledge the message they are giving you, then you begin to develop a very keen emotional intelligence. Sure, you have made a mistake, but here is an opportunity to take a few moments to reflect wisely and learn from it.

An aware student restrains any desire to justify or blame on account of those feelings and stays with them. An uncomfortable, guilty feeling does not arise from nowhere – there will be an associated memory of what took place. Having clearly comprehended the link between the result and the prior action, the student can then simply make a mental note to the effect that, given a similar situation in the future, they will endeavour to respond differently. All that is left to do is to stay with the feelings and mindfully watch as they start to fade away.

Beyond this there is nothing further to be done. You have performed an action and have experienced the natural result. There is no "Sword of Damocles" left dangling over you and no divine thumb ready to squash you out of existence, you are free to forget it and move on. If, from time to time, another memory of the same past action arises, there will be another painful feeling, but these are just further reverberations of that deed occurring in the mind-stream and they can be treated in exactly the same way.

Understanding the reality of *kamma* and *kamma-vipāka* and taking mindful responsibility for our behaviour in this way, can save us from a whole heap of unnecessary spiritual angst, guilt trips and possibly years of expensive psychoanalysis.

Developing an ethically mature and intelligent outlook is not easy. There are many difficulties that we face and the potential to fall into what in Buddhism we call "the woeful way" is real and great. Fortunately, when we begin the training, the path is very wide indeed. As long as our external behaviour is not too extreme we will be fine. We need, however, to bear in mind that, were we to go too close to the edge, then we risk falling into a deep and dark abyss from which it will take an awfully long time to emerge again. In that sense, keeping the precepts is a very real protection.

As we continue to cultivate our ethics, mindfulness and wisdom, the path naturally becomes narrower. Our awareness of what constitutes blameworthy behaviour becomes ever more subtle and even relatively unassuming breakages in the precepts are found to leave a dark mark in the mind stream. This can occur to the point where no-one else is even aware that something untoward has happened and yet, to us, it is obvious, precisely because we can read the signs. We experience the same kind of painful feeling and sense of regret.

So it is our own direct experience that narrows the path in terms of what we personally consider to be "good" and "bad" or "acceptable" and "unacceptable," it is not something enforced from without. When, inevitably, from time to time we are blamed, criticised or judged by others, we know where they are right and where they are mistaken and, in either case, we find that we remain relatively unruffled. There is no way by this stage in our development that they could possibly know us better then we know ourselves.

We find that when, occasionally, we do fall off the edge it is not too bad at all, it is more like falling of a street kerb and it is easy to just step back onto the path. Taking responsibility in this way means that we can enjoy lives that are far more harmonious and peaceful. Additionally, we develop compassion and equanimity with regard to other people's misdemeanours and tend not to enter into the blame game because we know where they are coming from. After all, the human condition is common to all of us.

Simply living an ethical life, however, can never produce complete freedom. You are still bound by the need to maintain vigilance and to act with restraint. Only with full enlightenment are you truly free, when all extremes and polar opposites have been transcended.

Then it is as if the path completely merges with the surrounding landscape. You are finally unbounded and free to live spontaneously as you wish, without any guilt or fear of falling at all. The root of all inefficient and unwholesome behaviour is ignorance and, once that veil has finally fallen, the need for any specific ethical restraint has gone.

Most people who realise enlightenment, however, choose to maintain a meditative discipline and an ethical lifestyle. Gotama said that he lived by the very training he taught and took *Dhamma* as his standard. This, he said, was for the purposes of ease of living here and now. There was no craving and no resistance of any kind, the enlightened mind is entirely harmless. It was simply his preference.

The Buddha compared the mind freed from all passionate resistance to the trackless flight of a bird. From time to time people may find fault with an enlightened being, blaming them for some perceived injustice or character flaw. He or she will be able to bear the accompanying painful feelings comfortably knowing full well that they are the results of actions long since past. They will also be able to clearly comprehend where such criticisms are valid and when it is just their accuser's own neurotic preoccupations being projecting on to them. Either way they cannot be trapped by other people's storylines anymore. The enlightened know that they hurt no-one. Their actions are blameless, lacking in all craving, hatred and delusion, they leave no karmic residue at all. They see the world as it really is, like a picture drawn on the surface of water.

Whatever Next!?

Henry Ford, the U.S. car pioneer, said this*: "I adopted the theory of reincarnation when I was twenty-six ... work is futile if we cannot utilise the experience we collect in one life, in the next. When I discovered reincarnation it was as if I'd found a universal plan. I realised there was a chance to work out my ideas, time was no longer limited, I was no longer a slave to the hands of the clock." He continued, "Genius is experience. Some seem to think it is a gift or talent but it is the fruit of long experience in many lives... The discovery of reincarnation put my mind at ease. I would like to communicate to others the calmness that the long view of life gives to us."

Rebirth is a fundamental principle of the Buddha's teaching. The views surrounding what happens when we die were the same in the Buddha's own day as they are now. In essence there are three main possibilities: one life and then oblivion, one life and then either eternal heaven or eternal damnation or, thirdly, an infinite series of lives. The Buddha maintained that it was

*Interview in the *"San Francisco Examiner"* (26 August 1928) *Henry Ford Quotes*. [Online]. Available from: http://en.wikiquote.org/wiki/Henry_Ford [Accessed 21 September 2014]

the third of these views that best reflects what actually happens and, because of this, living in conformity with this view will significantly reduce one's suffering.

People often ask for evidence of rebirth as a way of allowing them to have faith in it. This is difficult. It is impossible for science to determine whether conscious experiencing does continue after the death of the physical body precisely because no objective physical measurements of it can be made. Science, just as with all spheres of knowledge, does have limits.

There is, however, a large amount of anecdotal evidence available. A scholarly investigation worthy of special mention is *Twenty Cases Suggestive of Reincarnation* by the Canadian psychiatrist Dr Ian Stevenson. Over forty years he travelled the world collecting, analysing and testing more than three thousand accounts of children who claimed they could remember past lives.

Personal claims of out of body experiences during near-death experiences are notoriously difficult to authenticate, but one example that stands out is that of Canadian Pam Reynolds[**] who underwent brain surgery to remove a blood clot.

The surgical procedure required Pam's body temperature to be lowered to 60 °F (16 °C), her breathing and heartbeat stopped, and the blood drained from her head. Her eyes were closed with tape and small ear plugs with speakers were placed in her ears that emitted audible clicks which were used to check that she had a non-responsive brain. With no brain-wave activity and no blood flowing in her brain she was rendered clinically dead for part of the operation.

Yet after the surgery, Reynolds maintained that she remained conscious throughout and was able to accurately describe the

[**] Details retreived from Wikipedia (last update July 2014) *Pam Reynolds Case.* [Online]. Available from: http://en.wikipedia.org/wiki/Pam_Reynolds_case [Accessed: 21 September 2014]

procedure and the equipment that the surgeon used, as well as the conversations he had with his team members.

Does that constitute proof of life after death? No. The reality, however, is that none of us has very long to wait to find out the truth for ourselves, first-hand. The question is does that bother you? And do you realise just how much your belief affects the way you live your life?

The world is very unfair as seen from a one life perspective. There is no rhyme or reason as to why one person should be born rich, handsome and clever and another should be born poor, ugly and dim-witted. Life is assumed to be faulty and we must work like stink to try and redress the imbalance. Then, at the end of a lifetime of unremitting work and struggle, learning, exploring, creating and procreating, we face the agonising prospect of utter oblivion.

As Henry Ford's quote suggests, however, being open to the possibility of many lives changes everything. Is it possible that your current situation, whether you consider it to be positive or negative, is the result of your own behaviour? Is it conceivable that the conditions you met with at birth were the result of actions performed previously and that how you choose to behave now will determine the kind of future life you might experience?

Being open to this idea does mean that you have to take proper responsibility for how you behave, you can no longer simply blame your parents or the government or society for your unhappiness, but it also means that you become "captain of your ship" and that your future happiness is very much in your own hands.

As the Buddha suggested, faith and confidence in what he taught comes from applying the principles of his teaching in one's everyday life. Does one's suffering reduce through remaining open-minded to the possibility of more than one life?

Being open to the idea of rebirth is essential if we wish to reduce and eliminate suffering. It gives us a new, more tolerant perspective with which we can view the circumstances of our lives. This attitude leads to a more spacious and peaceful mind-set which allows for the development of unbiased observation of our subjective experience. It is through mindfulness that we come to comprehend clearly that it is always the passionate resistance to our circumstances that creates suffering, not the circumstances themselves. This knowledge then empowers us to bring suffering to an end.

This is why, when people ask me whether it is possible to follow the Buddha's Noble Eightfold Path without including rebirth, the answer is always no. To walk the path successfully you need to get your views straight and that means at the very least being open to the idea of many lives.

The Buddha said that were you to collect up the bones of every life you have already lived (if that were possible) the pile would end up being higher than Mount Everest. He also said that craving was the driving force behind renewed existence. It is our never-ending desire for conscious experience that prompts the creation of an endless series of bodies, bodies that inevitably decay and turn to dust, again and again.

Understanding rebirth is central to understanding the whole problem of suffering. To remove rebirth from the Buddha's teaching and still expect to reach the cessation of suffering is like removing the wheels from your car and still expect to drive to work.

The Buddha offered a simple way to look at this problem. He said that if you hold a view that life goes on after death and you live your life accordingly then, should it be that conscious experience does not continue, you will die knowing that you have lived a relatively good life, you will leave behind a positive legacy and you will not have lost anything that you were not going to lose anyway. Of course, if it transpires that experiencing does continue after death then, having lived well and in accordance with that view, a happy rebirth is the likely outcome. The reverse, however, is also applicable and one wonders what kind of shock someone who resolutely clings to a one life view would be in for if it turns out that the flow of conscious experiencing does actually continue in some shape or form after the break-up of the physical base.

★ ★ ★

The Buddha said that every aspect of what he taught can be discovered for oneself. Ultimately, the whole issue of rebirth is resolved through the practice of *vipassanā*. To gain insight-wisdom requires an open-minded attitude towards the idea of rebirth. If we hold to the idea of a durable, persisting self that is either annihilated at death or lives on eternally unchanged, then there comes a point when our views are contradicted by the evidence of our own experience. If we cling rigidly to those views no further insight is possible because we are forced to ignore that evidence.

Through *vipassanā* we come to see for ourselves that conscious experience arises and passes away moment by moment in a ceaseless but forever changing flow. It is said that you can never step in the same river twice and close observation of our subjective experience shows us that there is nothing permanent or unchanging in the flow of consciousness. There is no solid entity, no eternal self or conscious witness behind events and, therefore, nothing to die at all.

One comprehends directly that all the views that arise about what happens when we "die" are based on an assumption, the assumption that the way things appear to be is actually the way they really are. We discover that all our fears and the views they spawn concerning our mortality are unjustified, based as they are on wrong information.

Through generating insight-wisdom into transience and conditionality, the understanding blossoms that it is not a case of life versus death at all. You see clearly that, just as a coin has two sides, so life contains both birth and death within it. This same pattern is found in every element of existence and at every level, from moment to moment and throughout all the events and circumstances we encounter within this life and with each successive existence.

Everything arises and everything passes away again, mind and matter, consciousness, even time and space, but this process has no discernible beginning or end. Everything within life comes and goes, but life itself neither arises nor passes away, it is truly eternal.

Holy Smoke

Nibbāna is the goal of all authentic religious and spiritual traditions. It is gnosis, the complete, unimpeded and non-conceptual understanding of the way life really is. A single moment of perfect illumination that renders obsolete all of those unanswered questions with regard to existence, such as whether there is a creator God or a divine plan to life and whether or not we continue to exist after death. With the help of the Buddha's teaching and sufficient endeavour, it is possible for anyone to realise *nibbāna* themselves. The Buddha called his training *brahma-cariya* (the holy life) precisely because it leads to this "divine" or "pure" realisation.

Given the universal and transcendental nature of the goal and the roles that faith, devotion and surrender play in walking the path, a question often asked is whether or not Buddhism constitutes a religion.

Buddha-dhamma is fundamentally non-theistic and one of its core principles is that deliverance is only possible through individual effort. If we define religion "as a body of beliefs and practices regarding the supernatural and the worship of one or more deities" then strictly speaking Buddhism is not a religion.

This is because, although there are spiritual practices and a well defined belief system, there is no worship and most definitely no possibility of salvation through faith alone. One needs to investigate one's experience to generate insight-wisdom in order to destroy attachments first. Even attachment to the Buddha's own teaching has, ultimately, to be surrendered. The very system he devised is to be transcended.

Yet, visit traditional Buddhist countries and you find plenty of evidence of Buddhism meeting people's emotional needs by fulfilling the role of a traditional religion.

I remember, many years ago, standing outside a famous temple in Kandy, Sri Lanka and watching as a well-dressed man jumped off his moped, prostrated himself before the temple gates and started praying to the Buddha for a successful day at the office; well, that is what it looked like to me. I was somewhat surprised at the time because, for me, one of the great attractions of *buddha-dhamma* has always been the emphasis on personal investigation and verification through direct experience, with a definite absence of superstition and wishful thinking.

It all begins to make more sense, however, if we give religion a much broader definition, such as "something we put our faith, loyalty or devotion in to help us through the difficulties of life." Although this means that anything, football, music or even science could conceivably qualify as also being religion, none-the-less, it is in just this way that Buddhism is popularly used.

Further, it is clear that not everyone on this planet is consciously intent on realising *nibbāna*. Everyone has lessons to learn, but for most the idea of spiritual enlightenment is too remote a possibility to be taken seriously or just does not figure at all in their world-view.

What the majority of people want from a religious teaching is a clear ethical framework, so that they are able to live life well, here and now, with a reassurance about what will be in store for them when they die. In other words, they want enough of an explanation of things so that they can put their existential uncertainty to one side and get on with living life. So ceremony and ritual plays a central role in their lives as a way of reconfirming their faith in what they believe.

It is lovely to see genuine reverence and devotion openly displayed and people from traditionally Buddhist countries seem to have an innate understanding of how to perform rituals and ceremonies in gentle, unassuming ways. Singing, chanting, reciting holy verse, prostration and burning incense, these things can focus the mind and develop the intention to practise. They can also generate a peaceful and benevolent atmosphere, help to promote attitudes of piety, surrender and joy and instil a real community spirit and sense of being part of a deeply-rooted tradition. As such, ritual and ceremony can be useful. There are, however, also some very real dangers associated with them.

One point at issue is that all too easily the original intentions behind a ritual are lost and all that is left is the empty performance; the mere repetition of the form, with no substance at all. Further, with the passing of time, ritual form is mistakenly taken to be the real teaching. The inevitable conclusion is that well-meaning people come to believe that through the mere repetition of such outward displays along with the requisite degree of faith deliverance can be won. It cannot.

In Buddhism students traditionally take refuge in the *Buddha*, *Dhamma* and *Saṅgha* in the form of chanting in the ancient languages of Pali or Sanskrit. Recollecting these three "jewels" definitely does help to promote joy and confidence, and these are ideal states of mind to establish if you want to meditate. Confusion can arise, however, if people start to believe that reciting the chant is what it means to take refuge.

To take refuge in the *Buddha*, *Dhamma* and *Saṅgha* means to undertake the Buddha's Noble Eightfold Path in earnest. One is protected from the vicissitudes of life only by bringing one's behaviour in line with the way reality works. The belief that somehow the chanting itself is a protection is a false notion.

The Buddha explicitly rejected all forms of superstition. On one occasion, he criticised the popular idea that symbolic washing could possibly have the power to restore the individual to a state of purity. He quipped that if people could wash away their sins by bathing in sacred rivers, then all the turtles, crocodiles and frogs would go to heaven. The mind is polluted by negative thoughts and unethical behaviour. No amount of humble supplication will ever be enough without the cultivation of the three trainings in ethical conduct, mental control and wisdom to remove ignorance and craving. He called this the "inner washing."

Attachment to rule and ritual represents a very real block to meditative insight. It is rightly called a fetter, because it binds a person so tightly to the endless cycle of suffering. There must be the willingness to investigate your own subjective experience and this means mindfully acknowledging aspects of life and your nature that you have always tried to hide from. This is very challenging work and can be fearful and painful at times too, which is why developing attitudes of faith and devotion is so important.

One can quite understand why people through doubts, fear, laziness or other misgivings might prefer to defer from real practice, contenting themselves with religious pomp and ceremony, lulling themselves into believing that what they are doing is deeply meaningful and taking them in the right direction. The reality, however, beyond a certain level, is that reliance on ritual form is just sheer wishful thinking.

If our habitual behaviour is ritualistic in nature, it means we tend to do things over and over in a "bull at a gate" type way, forever performing the same action, yet forever expecting a different result. We want one rule for all occasions, ostensibly so that we do not have to bother to think for ourselves or go through the pain of learning. To live happily and successfully, however, requires that we be flexible to all of life's demands, by learning to take note of prevailing conditions and becoming skilful at adapting our approach to suit.

This is especially true when it comes to meditation. The sad irony of attachment to rule and ritual is that it has the effect of inflating and reinforcing the very pride and self-regard that undertaking spiritual practices was supposed to be reducing. It strengthens the sense of duality, the sense of "me" as an entity separate from the rest of life, making us ever more stubborn, inflexible and resistant to change. This consequently takes us further away than ever from truth and freedom.

If we go too far down the route of religious worship then the goal of the Buddha's teaching is placed on such a high pedestal that people no longer believe it to be a realistic aim. I have read articles in Buddhist magazines that suggest the best we can hope for in our modern era is to refine our ethical behaviour and wait for more suitable conditions in a future life to realise *nibbāna*. This idea is sad because it unwittingly reduces enlightenment itself to myth and superstition, as well as implying that the Noble Eightfold Path is not effective in certain conditions, none of which is true. Enlightenment is real and available right here, right now. People can and do find it. The Buddha's Four Noble Truths are timeless and the path is currently available and supremely effective.

★ ★ ★

While the Buddha was lying on his deathbed, a monk continued to meditate rather than going to pay him homage. When he heard of this the Buddha praised the monk saying: "He honours me best, who practises my teaching the best."

Those genuinely intent on realising *nibbāna* need to keep a proper sense of proportion by recognising the limited value of rule and ritual, and understanding the difference between real practice and superstition. By restraining the urge to raise the goal up to unattainable levels, we can remain open to the truth that the answer lies very close to home and is most definitely within reach, but only if one's approach to the training is genuinely sincere, devoted and humble.

Letting the World Go Free

A bird-feeder is suspended from the branch of a tree close to the house that you can watch from your window. Packed full of nuts, the feeder not only attracts birds but also squirrels, which, with typical cunning, have learned how to undo the screw that keeps the base of the feeder on. Occasionally, you find the patio strewn with remnant nuts and an empty bird-feeder swinging gently in the breeze. The squirrels' antics and their resourcefulness are usually very amusing. Today, however, you bear witness to their suffering.

In attempting to undo the screw on the bird-feeder one of them has got his tail caught in the wire from which the feeder is suspended. Hanging upside-down he is furiously arching his back trying to reach up and untangle himself, but the tail is simply too long. He is well and truly stuck.

So the question is what do you do? Perhaps the obvious and compassionate choice would be to go out and try to help the squirrel. Is that, however, really the best thing to do? I have, myself, witnessed this very scenario and the appalling results. The squirrel reacted as any animal would. He did not see a kindly Buddhist coming to his rescue, he only knew that he was trapped and believed he faced certain death if he did not escape. In a burst of frenzy and in abject fear for his life, the squirrel twisted his body so furiously that he completely severed the trapped part of his tail and, free at last, scampered off as fast as he could. So, faced with that possibility, is it better not to intervene? In which case, given how completely caught up he is, in all likelihood the squirrel will hang to death.

The Buddha stated categorically that "life is suffering" and this being so ethical conundrums like this are bound to arise. When your teenage son is clearly about to do something extremely foolish, should you intervene to help him avoid unnecessary pain or let him make the mistake and hope he learns from it? When another country is in the grip of civil war, how should our government respond? Support the regime? Arm the rebels? Invade? Or do nothing and watch a whole nation implode?

There are no easy answers. Life is not black or white. Our decisions do count and our actions are bound to impact on others. Even when our decision is not to act, that will still have an effect. We are individual elements connected within the whole; the way the part behaves affects the whole and the movement of the whole affects each part.

Although we have no option as to whether our actions have an impact on the world, we do have choices as to what kind of impact they might have. To know what is truly in our own or another's best interest requires real life experience. Such wisdom is developed through the attempt to live an ethical life.

To practise *sīla* requires us to generate mindfulness and through the generation of mindfulness we become far more conscious of our desires, intentions and actions in response to life's difficulties and, critically, the results they bring.

Practising *sīla*, therefore, helps to keep us safe because, as our understanding of the mundane world becomes more subtle and refined, especially the law of *kamma*, so our choices become wiser and life becomes more harmonious.

Generating mindfulness also conditions a natural compassion for others because with the greater clarity we begin to really appreciate how much everyone suffers. Knowing, however, what is in another's best interest and wishing that they be free of suffering is not enough. In addition to wisdom and compassion we also need equanimity.

Equanimity is not coldness, indifference or apathy. Neither is it just being a door-mat and it does not in any way preclude action to solve a problem or to change a situation.

Equanimity is the even-minded acceptance of reality as it presents itself at any given moment, free from any passionate response. As such, it is the opposite of resistance, craving for things to be different.

In the example of the squirrel hanging helplessly from the wire, the *dukkha* inherent in that situation is obvious and it is only natural to wish the little critter freedom from his predicament. Resistance is the non-acceptance of the unfolding reality. It is the voice that says, "This should not be happening." This leads to clinging attachment, which is the reinforcement of that craving with justifications and condemnations, comparisons and expectations. It is here that ignorant assumptions become cast-iron and passionately held views and opinions. It is where idealism and extremism are born, all of which is in opposition to reality.

To practise the Buddha's way is to fully acknowledge the *dukkha* inherent in the situation and to feel genuine compassion, but compassion that is accompanied by an even-minded acceptance of the facts of reality. Equanimity comes from understanding the fundamental laws of life, such as the first noble truth that suffering in life is unavoidable and the second that to respond by craving only creates further *dukkha*. After all, life could not be different than it is right now.

Perhaps, in some parallel universe, the squirrel has decided to forage for food somewhere else today or perhaps you had not restocked the bird-feeder recently. In this universe, however, right here, right now, the squirrel is in the predicament he is in. That is the reality. We suffer whenever we are at odds with reality.

Where no resistance arises, no subsequent clinging attachment arises either and, in the absence of any passionate clinging, you are free to make your choice to intervene or not intervene as you see fit. In either case the result will be what it will be. After all, how can we possibly predict how, say, the squirrel will react? What is important is the motivation behind our choice.

The law of *kamma* is such that actions taken with a view of self always produce a result, but whether that result is bitter or sweet is dependent on the understanding and motivation behind the action. This is not to imply that the squirrel will not suffer if you act with the correct motivation. The actions you perform produce results for you to experience, the squirrel is a being in his own right and has his own *kamma* and *kamma-vipāka*, he has his own lessons to learn.

In reality there is no absolute right or wrong choice for every occasion. There are an infinite number of conditions operating at any one time, so you cannot live life "by numbers." Meditation students are encouraged to let go of their idealism, to treat each new situation on its merits and to be mindful of their own desires, intentions and responses to all of life's difficulties.

The more we see through our own experience that life is entirely transient, conditioned and uncontrollable, the more we let go of idealism and extreme views of all kinds. The more we allow life to be what it is without passionately craving for it to be different, the less we suffer. Such wisdom breeds greater compassion because we see that the suffering world around us is still entirely caught up in resisting life. That compassion may well inspire us to action, but all such action is balanced by the personal knowledge that beings fare along according to their deeds. They must be allowed the freedom to experience the results of their actions in order to learn, just as we have.

It cannot be stressed enough, however, that the perfect consummation of wisdom and compassion, enlightenment, cannot occur whilst there is still the merest trace of clinging attachment to the world. To transcend the world you must first let it go free. That is to say that you must allow it to be exactly what it is, free from any idealistic interference.

How Meditation Brings You to Your Senses

Over the last century or so our society has largely operated on the premise that the more you consume the happier you will be. Has this experiment worked? For a while it seemed that you really could have your cake and eat it, but it turns out, after all, that you cannot.

At the time of writing this book the world is going through a period of great uncertainty, convulsing with wave upon wave of evermore dramatic calamity: global debt, ecological disaster, political upheaval and breakdowns in civil order spreading from country to country. Are people happier? A small minority are definitely much richer, that is for sure. These days, however, it seems that even with the latest and greatest technological advances, people are more worried than ever about the future. Why is the world in such a parlous state?

A criticism I once heard levelled at modern western spiritual teachers and writers was that, while they were very willing to talk about how to overcome the problem of hatred, few seemed to discuss in detail that other all-consuming mental cancer, that of greed. In an out and out materialist society the "G" word is the one that no-one wants to hear. It is too uncomfortable because the unconscious assumption that happiness comes from self-gratification fundamentally underpins so many people's aspirations in life.

The Buddha talked about there being a middle way between extremes. We would all like a reasonable level of material comfort and security, but are these global problems a result of having gone too far?

Natural resources like rainforests and fossil fuels are being consumed at an alarmingly fast rate, industrial expansion continues to pollute the earth's ecosystem and now the planet is so warm that the polar ice caps are melting. Have we gone too far? It would seem so.

Advertising is continually encouraging us to purchase goods and services only a few can genuinely afford, we are encouraged to gratify our desires by splashing out now and paying later. The debt that is inevitably created is even considered to be a sellable commodity and ripe for profit. Have we gone too far? It would seem so.

In a world where obesity is rampant, my local fish and chip shop sells chips in "regular," "large" and "American" size portions and the regular size alone is enough for two people. Have we gone too far? It would seem so.

The trouble with consumption as a way to happiness is that it does not work. Okay, there may be a fleeting happiness or contentment when our desires are sated. The reality, however, is that sensual pleasures are like salty water – the more you drink the thirstier you get. Indulgence stimulates desire. The effects of indulgence are extremely brief so you need to keep consuming to assuage those desires. There is also the fear of not being able to service those needs; just look at how far governments go to ensure that the precious supply of gas and oil is not disrupted. The Buddha stated emphatically that one of the outcomes of unchecked greed is warfare.

Buddhism is apolitical. It does not take sides because under-pinning the whole training is the enlightened understanding that life could not be different than it is, right now. Clearly there are lessons for everyone to learn with regard to the payback for acting with extreme greed but, as the saying goes, "You can lead a horse to water, but you cannot make it drink." The Buddhist meditator, understanding the facts of the matter, does not at-tempt to police everyone else's behaviour, but chooses instead to do something about the greed rooted in his or her own nature in a peaceful way.

The Buddha encouraged meditators to practise renunciation. For people with a greedy nature this is another word they do not like to hear. As Tapussa the householder once said to the Buddha, "Venerable sir, we are householders who indulge in sensuality, delight in sensuality, enjoy sensuality and rejoice in sensuality. For us, renunciation is like jumping off a cliff."

In reply, the Buddha said that it was necessary to see the genu-ine drawbacks in worldly desires. This then leads naturally to an understanding of the rewards of renunciation. The Buddha said that becoming familiar with such rewards, "The meditator's heart leaps up at renunciation, grows confident, steadfast and firm, seeing it as peace."

What is renunciation? It is the willingness to make an intel-ligent sacrifice. An intelligent sacrifice is one where you gain a greater happiness by letting go of a lesser one; in the same way that you would give up a bag of sweets if offered a pot of gold in exchange.

Practising renunciation can be done in many different ways and permeates the whole of the Noble Eightfold Path. Keeping the five Buddhist precepts, practising generosity, moderation in eating, having fewness of wishes and being content with little are all forms of renunciation. At a more subtle level it includes practising sense-restraint, whereby the meditator is careful, for example, about how much time they spend surfing the internet or window shopping and the like. Renunciation also includes time spent with eyes closed in meditation and more subtle yet, it includes the willingness to refrain from allowing the mind to wallow in sensual fantasy and other pleasure seeking thoughts.

Through practice, meditators are able to compare the resultant mind-states that arise through their experience of indulging or restraining the senses. They find that indulging sense-desires results in a distracted mind that is constantly looking outward and lacks the ability to focus. They recognise quite how discontented and listless they consequently feel, how that lessens their resolve to practise meditation and increases their desire to indulge further. They also begin to appreciate quite how much time, energy and expense is required to continually service desires and how pointless and never ending that process is.

Conversely, through learning to restrain the urge to indulge the senses, the meditator experiences an absence of restlessness. The mind is able to concentrate so much more easily. There is a perception of having plenty of time in daily life generally which creates a sense of spaciousness and a keenness to engage in more meditation, as well as an overall sense of well-being and self-esteem. Paradoxically such all round restraint of the senses gives us a greater appreciation of the immense beauty and mystery of life that occurs naturally all around us. Life becomes its own reward and no longer requires so much artificial stimulation.

In developing renunciation, students must be sure not to fall into the trap of trying to deny themselves any of life's little luxuries in the misunderstanding that it must all be bad. The Buddha said that wherever and however happiness is found that is indeed happiness. The idea is to make intelligent sacrifices based on an appreciation of why the sacrifices are being made. The line to take is to find the middle ground between the extremes of too much and too little. It would be counterproductive to deny ourselves access to the cultural norms in which we live. There is nothing wrong with owning a television, for instance, but we might limit the amount we watch. Learning to defer gratification is a very good discipline. To get the maximum enjoyment from something it does make sense to do it less frequently.

In the final analysis greed is an entirely destructive force, creating the most terrible suffering. Unchecked and rampant it ultimately always leads to corruption, humiliation and ruination. People entirely caught up with attachment to finding pleasure and avoiding pain at all costs are slaves to their senses and, therefore, to suffering.

The classic analogy is of a clever hunter who sets a trap for a monkey by putting honeycomb in the hollow of a tree. The monkey comes along and puts his hand in the hollow to take out the honeycomb, but the hollow is too small to take out his hand and the honeycomb together. If the monkey lets go, he is free, but his greed does not allow him to do so. He wants the honeycomb so much he cannot bear to let go of it and, therefore, of his own choosing, he remains stuck and at the mercy of the hunter.

Grasping sensory experiences in an attempt to find lasting happiness is like grasping handfuls of sand. Ultimately, there is nothing lasting or truly satisfying in any sensory experience and the failure to notice this is what drives the wheel of *saṃsāra*. The way off the wheel is to let go of the attachment to sense-pleasures and this can only be done by paying proper attention to reality.

In *vipassanā* meditation the objective is to observe what the Buddha called the six-sensory fields: those of eye, ear, nose, tongue, body and mind and to investigate their true nature. This is so as to see clearly that there really is nothing in all of conscious experience that can be grasped after.

No sensory contact lasts; it is all fleeting, insubstantial and unsatisfactory. As a meditator perfects his view and intuitively comprehends that there really is nothing of substance in any of the six sensory fields, his attachment to sense-pleasures naturally falls away. In place of the constant thirst for more sense experience and the restlessness conditioned by such attachment, the mind is quiet, peaceful and happy. The madness of greed is finally at an end.

Solitude

Traditional accounts have it that after many hundreds of thousands of lifetimes preparing to fulfil his role as an historical Buddha, the *bodhisatta* (the Buddha-to-be) took up his final living form as Prince Siddhartha Gotama. It is said that during his long round of rebirths he developed boundless compassion for beings and a comprehensive understanding of how conventional existence works. In his last life he dedicated himself to realising the transcendental or supramundane wisdom of *nibbāna*. Upon his enlightenment he was, as a result, blessed with a complete knowledge of life, both how to live most effectively in the world, and how, ultimately, to transcend it altogether. The culmination of his endeavours, the Four Noble Truths and the Noble Eightfold Path, balances the natural human instinct for social integration with the need for solitude and deeper investigation into life.

Some people mistakenly believe that working towards their own enlightenment is somehow selfish. They think that the ideal of Buddhism should be to dedicate oneself entirely to helping relieve the suffering of others, without regard for oneself. This, however, is not, what the Buddha taught. There are undoubtedly times when seeking solitude and detachment from the wider world would be inappropriate, when war is on one's doorstep, for instance. Other than in such extreme cases, however, it is perfectly permissible for people to seek solitude to deepen their understanding of life.

After his countless lifetimes of developing wisdom, the Buddha understood that suffering can never be eradicated through external action alone. Realising that the true cause of suffering was an internal matter, that of craving, he maintained that mindfulness was the one way to understanding. He, therefore, instructed his monks to find solitude in nature, to be in the wildernesses and seek out empty places where they could practise without being disturbed.

Although living in a forest as a penniless mendicant recluse isn't really possible in our culture and climate, there are still plenty of ways to find solitude. If it is the case that someone has not yet committed to marriage, family and career and if they are free of debt, are in good health and are not wanted by the police, then training as a full-time recluse in a Buddhist monastery provides the best possible conditions for practice.

For those whose circumstances do not allow that level of involvement, solitude can still be found through attending regular week-long silent retreats where such conditions are replicated. Solitude can, however, be found by anyone on a daily basis, for, whenever we sit down with eyes closed to meditate, that itself is the practice of solitude.

Before I entered into full-time training, wherever I went to work I always managed to find a nearby park to sit and have my lunch, and this gave me at least a little time and space for mindfulness and quiet reflection.

One can only really be comfortable and happy in solitude, however, if your relationship with the rest of life is harmonious. This requires of meditators to live an ethical life, which means paying attention to their outward behaviour and ensuring that it is as harmless as possible. Keeping the precepts, therefore, engaging in *pāramī* (compassionate activities), especially developing *mettā* (friendliness to all beings), are integral aspects of the Noble Eightfold Path and essential to the meditator's overall aim of realising freedom from suffering. You cannot transcend a world that you are still at odds with.

In recent years the phrase *"engaged* Buddhism" has been coined as a way to stress the importance of driving forward social change. This, however, is an unnecessary adjunct as the Buddha's teaching is already entirely engaged. Seeking solitude is not at all the same thing as hiding away and being indifferent to the suffering around us. Living an ethical life is undertaken on an ongoing basis in concurrence with meditation.

Solitude is not isolation. In reality, you cannot divorce yourself from the rest of the world no matter how hard you try. Sitting alone in a mountain cave without access even to a mobile signal, you are still utterly connected to your world. After all, let us not forget that *nibbāna* is the realisation that reality is and has always been non-dual and empty of any division.

So many people seem to be wary of solitude and choose to cram their lives full of useful or interesting things to do, or constantly seek out entertainment and distraction. Even a day out rambling in the country-side can so easily become a chatterbox's jamboree. There seems to be such an investment in constant conversation, in expressing oneself and airing one's precious views and opinions. It is as if to simply sit or walk without continuous verbal babbling is somehow a failing. And how uncomfortable people feel during one of those awkward silences when, for once, no-one can think of anything to say. Yet, in reality, how much of what is spoken is even vaguely important? Would the world actually end if, perhaps, what you felt in such urgent need of expressing was actually left unsaid? Furthermore, what peculiar force is it that propels such constant verbal diarrhoea?

The answer, conversely, is the same reason why those who are committed to realising enlightenment actively seek solitude, that of ignorance and craving. Whenever we become truly quiet, we start to become aware of life as it really is and this can often feel very uncomfortable. Unschooled in the workings of our subjective experience we distrust, or even fear, our own company. There is little or no understanding of how our minds operate and even less understanding of the inherent emptiness at the heart of life. It is no wonder, therefore, that fear emerges, prompting us to create the "white-noise" of constant chatter and diversion as a way of ignoring reality.

The meditator seeks out solitude not out of hatred for life, but to discover it. He or she forsakes the worldly ways of chatter, entertainment and distraction precisely to experience that awkward, uncomfortable silence. Through experiencing it they come to understand it for what it is and overcome any fear of it.

As well as the external chatter, the internal mental chatter of constant narration, judgement and comparison is also sacrificed. The meditator learns how to "pluck the world out of the mind" and comes to understand that the quiet mind is not an enemy, such inner solitude is truly delightful. The quiet mind is at peace with its surroundings and at peace with itself. It is the window through which deep insights into the nature of life are received and comprehended.

Solitude is not loneliness. Loneliness is a form of suffering born of comparison and wanting life to be different than it is. Much of a person's sense of alienation can be removed by undertaking the Buddha's mundane training. Ultimately, through learning to calm and quieten the mind you come to realise that you are never alone because, in reality, there is no separation anywhere at all. The quiet mind is quiet precisely because there is no self-concern. States of mind such as loneliness or a sense of abandonment are devilish tactics the ego conjures up to ensure that the delusion of selfhood is maintained at all costs. So much of our mental chatter is simply there to reinforce the self-enclosing wall of ignorance. It is only the quiet mind, the mind that enjoys this inner solitude, that can see what lies beyond that wall.

★ ★ ★

You wake up at dawn, unzip the tent and take in the view. What a beautiful morning! You look down into the valley where the sun is just beginning to bathe the rolling hills in its gentle morning light. A delicate white mist hangs above the river below, giving the scene an air of mystery. Everything is so still and peaceful. There is no breeze. It all looks so enchanting and, as no-one else is around yet, you decide to go for a walk down to the river.

You quietly descend through a field of tall golden grasses and colourful wild flowers marvelling at their fragile beauty. For a little while you follow a deep, ancient track and carefully pick your way over the huge, gnarled roots of the old trees that line the route. Still nothing stirs until you hear a rustling in the undergrowth and turning quickly catch a brief glimpse of what you fancy might be a badger. The rustling stops instantly and wary of frightening the creature, whatever it may be, after a brief pause you carry on your way.

A tiny village nestles at the river's edge and you stand on a stone bridge watching as plumes of mist rise from the surface of the water, coalesce and drift quietly a few meters above the river. Although there is a strong current below, the river surface appears still and perfectly mirrors the white mist, the blue sky beyond and the green of the trees and vegetation on the river bank. Someone in the village must have a dovecote because nine pure white doves are circling in wide arcs around you, in perfect silent harmony.

These pictures, these fragile pictures, come together in one moment of perfect silent harmony and are gone – and that is all there is. There is no solidity, no real substance. It is all a mirage, empty of any intrinsic, separate existence. It is so delightful to understand emptiness, the emptiness of form. It is magical, mysterious and you cannot capture it. Understanding emptiness is total immersion in life. There is no "you" separate from the picture, there is just the coming together and dissolution of the picture and this is timeless perfection. To realise emptiness is to know what love really is.

Learning to Breathe

The Buddha's teaching is designed to help us find freedom from all restless seeking and the ignorance that causes it. The Buddha maintained that the "one way" to do that was through mindfulness. Mindfulness is a window of awareness that you create by consciously restraining craving and developing the capacity to remain settled and alert in the moment. This in turn allows you to observe the wonderfully evolving mystery of life that has been going on right under your nose but unnoticed the whole time. To help us accomplish this, the Buddha taught a method called *ānāpānasati* which means Mindfulness of Breathing.

The breath is a most wondrous, life sustaining process, running quite automatically, day and night, supplying oxygen to the body and removing carbon dioxide from it. For the most part, however, it is something that we take utterly for granted. Being mindful of the breathing process, though, can show us incredible things about the way in which life actually works.

Someone once asked me how it was possible to become wise just by watching the breath. Wisdom arises from experiencing life as it really is. Watching the breathing process unfold is watching life unfold, and the direct understanding of the fundamental characteristics of life is what we call wisdom. Everyone has the capacity to watch the breath and therefore everyone has the potential to be wise.

Learning to watch the breath mindfully also helps to develop a whole host of other beneficial mental qualities, such as the capacity for deep concentration and focus, intent, tranquillity, equanimity and fascination. As a result of learning to watch the breath, you naturally tend to be much more enthralled with what is happening in your immediate experience, not just during meditation but also at other times too.

The breath is a very suitable object for developing mindfulness, which is why the Buddha chose it. It is always freely available, you do not have to carry it around in your pocket and you are not going to lose the breath like you might sometimes lose your car-keys. The breath is a neutral object, that is to say one which is unlikely either to over-stimulate the mind or make it irritable or dull. As everyone knows, observing the breath does help you calm down. If you are anxious then people will always recommend that you take a few deep breaths. Watching the breath has, therefore, this capacity to ground us and bring us back to reality.

There are different ways you can watch the breath. Some people teach watching the whole of the breath, coming from the movement of the diaphragm, all the way up through the lungs, up into the throat, up through and out of the nose and then all the way back in again. Other people suggest just observing the breath as it enters and leaves the tip of the nostrils. Here at the House of Inner Tranquillity we teach the observation of what is essentially the movement of the abdomen that occurs due to the breathing process.

In principle one can develop concentration by giving your undivided attention to pretty much any object and so one way of observing the breath is not necessarily better than another. As it happens, though, attending to the movement of the abdomen encourages deep breathing which is very healthy, but that is really a side benefit. The most important thing is to choose one object for contemplation and be prepared to stick to it through thick and thin.

How do you practise mindfulness of breathing? To provide a solid foundation for meditation it is important to live life in an ethical and relatively blameless way. It also helps tremendously to have a reasonably quiet and tidy secluded place to practise.

The first thing, then, is to set a timer so that you will not be distracted during the session with thoughts about how long there is left to go. A daily half-hour session is usually manageable for most people to begin with.

As for posture, sitting cross-legged is not strictly necessary. For most westerners, sitting in a chair is far more comfortable and sustainable. What is important, however, is to have a straight spine. If the back starts to droop it interferes with the flow of the breathing, so you want your rib cage to be up a bit, but you do not want the posture to be forced. Inevitably when we are sitting in meditation the head does tend to drop a little due to gravity and it is okay to lift it very gently up again, but other than that it is important not to move. As we practise mindfulness of breathing with eyes closed, keeping the back straight is also an important aid to wakefulness.

When we begin the session we need first of all need firmly to establish mindfulness. Many people just rush in thinking, "All right, I've got half an hour, I need to make every moment count." They just zoom straight in to watching the breath and within a few moments they are either very tense or fast asleep. A session of half an hour, or an hour, is plenty of time. It pays to make haste slowly by going into the meditation gradually and first establishing a general level of mindfulness.

It is very helpful to ask yourself questions such as, "What can I hear? What can I sense in my body? What is the current state of the mind?" or "What is going to happen next?" and then observe your experience without any preconception about what should or should not be happening.

If, for instance, you are meditating after work then it is very likely that there will be lots of thoughts about work. The mind wants to throw up all these thoughts, memories and perceptions to get rid of them, so it makes sense to stay alert and, with a non-judgmental outlook, give the mind time to settle. This in turn also gives the body a chance to become more peaceful and settled. Once you feel mindful, balanced and alert, then you can turn the attention to the sensation of the rise and fall of the breath.

There is no special breathing technique to employ, we just breathe normally. What, though, is normal breathing? There really is no such thing. The breath is always changing. This is one of the things that you come to see fairly quickly when you start practising *ānāpānasati*; breathing at one time is not the same as breathing at another.

Perhaps it is coarse and fast with the heart-rate quite high when you start the meditation, but sometime later the body has settled so that it does not need so much oxygen going round the system and the breathing just becomes naturally shallower. Then maybe you start thinking about something, perhaps a hindrance to meditation like sensual-desire or irritation pops up, and suddenly the heartbeat is going a little quicker and the breath has changed again. Other times you cannot detect the breath at all and some people think they must have died. If you have a similar thought when meditating, it helps just to bear in mind that if you are asking the question at all, then in all likelihood you are not dead.

Being caught up in such thinking is just one potential obstacle to the process of observing the breath. There are many different things that interfere with the simple process of just observing the breath: sense-desire, ill-will, sloth, worry and doubt to name but a few. Most of the problems, however, are resolved if we get the basic attitude towards mindfulness of breathing right.

The right attitude is to be totally interested in the breathing, which means that you are not at all interested in what watching the breathing will give you. If you are forever concerned about whether you are getting calm or whether insights are on the horizon or whether you are doing it properly or whether you are not doing it properly, the mind will never get calm. You will never reach that point of rest, that point of contentment that comes with mindfulness of breathing.

Imagine, for example, that you are sitting on your sofa at home snuggling up with your loved one watching a film on TV. Your loved one starts asking, "Am I doing it right? Am I doing it right? Am I watching this film correctly?" You think, "You mad person! What on earth are you going on about? Those are crazy things to say."

That is often, however, what we do in the meditation, isn't it? We wonder if we are correctly watching the breath. You do not sit down to watch a movie, though, in order to be really good at watching a movie. You do so to get engrossed in the movie, to the point that you forget that you are even watching a movie. Do you see the difference? It is the same with watching the breath, it is taking total interest in the breath itself to the exclusion of everything, to the point where there is no perception that you are meditating at all because the interest is totally on the breathing.

Becoming fascinated in the breath, initially, is not easy and it can help to artificially generate interest. One way of doing so is to estimate the characteristics of the breath.

Say you begin a meditation and you are a little out of breath and the heart is pumping fast, you can note to yourself that the breathing is short and fast. Then, as the body begins to settle down the breathing gradually lengthens and slows down, this change can be noted. As the body really starts to calm down and the heart beat slows, the breath becomes very small and also quiet.

As you progress you can also begin to detect other characteristics of the breathing. Sometimes it is coarse, sometimes it is fine, sometimes it is jagged, sometimes it is smooth, sometimes it is quite warm and other times it feels cold. Sometimes you perceive the breath as an up and down motion, whereas other times as an in and out motion or as an expansion and contraction. When there is an inhalation perhaps it normally feels like everything is moving up, but then you might perceive that there are muscles which are actually moving down at the same time. Do you get the idea? You are just so immersed in observing the breathing process that you forget about everything else, including the fact that you are meditating.

If you are taking a real interest in the breathing process, then when distracting thoughts arise they are not a problem at all. Have you ever, for example, had the experience of working on a project that you really do not want to do? You just want to do it to get rid of it. If then someone has the temerity to ask you a question you immediately snap at them. Whereas, when you are really enjoying what you are doing and someone interrupts you, you really do not mind at all. After the disruption, of course, all you are going to do is just go back to something you were really taking a pleasure in. It is the same with meditation. If you are enjoying what you are doing then disturbances never need become distractions.

Through training the mind to take an interest in the breathing process a natural fascination begins to emerge. It also brings a sense of well-being, a lovely feeling of happiness and rapture that wells up from deep within and pervades the whole body. Both mind and body start to feel extraordinarily light, spacious and tranquil. It becomes even easier, therefore, to let go of distracting

thoughts, feelings and sensations. As a result you remain beautifully even-minded and can focus effortlessly on the rise and fall
of the breath.

Once you get to this level of mindfulness you have a choice
to make. You can continue to develop and deepen levels of
concentration through observing the breath to the exclusion of
everything else. This is what in Buddhism we call *samatha* or
calming meditation. Alternatively, you can use mindfulness of
the breath to generate insight-wisdom which we call *vipassanā*.
The Buddha recommended both because both result in kinds of
freedom.

The freedom that comes with *samatha* is a calm, restful state
of mind. It is the freedom, for a while, from any resistance to life
whatsoever. It is blissful, peaceful and deeply alluring and there
is a strong sense of unity and connection to the universe. It is a
joy to experience. There is only one drawback and that is that it
is temporary. The effects will last for a little while after you have
meditated, but in order to get those effects back you have to keep
working at developing the mindfulness and concentration. That
is one kind of freedom.

The other freedom comes through practising *vipassanā* and
developing insight-wisdom into the truly transient, unsatisfactory and selfless nature of the breath and all other possible experiences. *Vipassanā* leads to an understanding that is transcendent
to the flow of conscious experience. This understanding ends
all existential angst and psychological dependency. It is also
blissful and happy, but in a sublime way that surpasses even the
most vaunted state of concentration. This understanding is not
transient; it does not come and go. It is, therefore, permanent,
undying freedom.

Making Friends with Your Demons

In the Holburne Art Museum in Bath you will find an oil painting of the Anchorite recluse St Anthony by the Flemish artist
Jan van de Venne. This third century hermit spent years in the
Egyptian desert where he suffered violent temptations in the
form of imaginary demons and erotic fantasies.

In van de Venne's painting the aged saint is shown kneeling
outside a cave clasping his hands in prayer, while a crouch-
ing demon nearby mimics his gestures. A lusty young woman
dressed in white beckons him and another older woman clutches
a money bag, trying to tempt him back to the material world.
Various other grotesque demons surround the monk including
one creature with a second head dripping down from its nose.

After his death, St Anthony's battles with temptation in the
desert became fable. His tormented hallucinations were reinter-
preted as real, external demons and with each retelling the stories
became ever more dramatic and bizarre. It is no wonder that
such lurid tales subsequently inspired artworks by the likes of
Hieronymus Bosch and Salvador Dali.

Everyone has inner demons of one sort or another. They are just
another name for our neurotic tendencies, such as fear, paranoia,

loneliness, passion, rage, restlessness, anxiety and doubt. States of mind like these are reflections of our continuing struggle to come to terms with the world being the way it is and our existence within it.

Battling with our demons is distressing and confusing, and leads to all kinds of complexities in our lives. Our inner conflicts are also externalised and projected outward. We see them represented in the arts and in literature, we see them being played out before our eyes each evening on the television news.

Learning how to deal with our inner demons is fundamental to all authentic spiritual traditions. Is it, perhaps, the truest meaning of the *jihad* or holy war? Viewing Jan van de Venne's painting as a practicing Buddhist I feel a strong empathy with St Anthony's plight.

In Buddhism these demons are not, however, regarded as the dastardly emissaries of some spiteful, envious devil, rather they are the products of our own minds. We create the monsters of greed, hatred and confusion ourselves. As we are personally responsible for their existence, we also, consequently, have it within our power to overcome them.

Anyone who has earnestly tried to meditate will have witnessed for themselves how these demons can turn what was supposed to be a mind-calming exercise into a torrid battleground. My own earliest attempts at meditation were so riddled with dreamy, sensual fantasy that my inner world often looked like it had been painted by Salvador Dali himself. Trying manfully to resist those surreal fantasies only seemed to strengthen their hold over my mind. Understandably this led to irritation, self-doubt and despondency, because the perceived lack of success made me feel bad.

If I did get any kind of insight during those early days it was that the popular notion of meditation just being an escape from the "real world" was laughable. It was clear that these mental monsters were a real problem and that their influence was felt in almost everything I did in life. Now, through developing sufficient mindfulness, I was becoming aware of the real damage that they were causing.

Meditation is not escapism, meditation is a reality check. If you are practising insight meditation correctly you are brought face to face with your demons. The whole emphasis in *vipassanā* is to overcome them, not through force or suppression, but by accepting their existence and watching carefully. In doing so you come to understand how you create them, hold on to them and keep them in being. You cannot do that if you are in denial of them or believe that they should not be there.

Sometimes, while we are watching the breath rise and fall, we experience boredom or a sense of guilt because we fear that we are not being productive. Sometimes we might become apprehensive just because everything goes quiet or perhaps we experience some physical discomfort or restlessness.

Trying to get away from the discomfort of these experiences we indulge in further resistances like sexual fantasy, irritation or doubt. As a consequence we become aware that our minds are now overrun with more undesirable, unwholesome thoughts and painful mental feelings; the polar opposite of the lovely, quiet, serene meditation we had hoped for.

This comparison between our ideal and the reality creates yet more resistance. It produces a complete misapplication of our energies as our mind is caught endlessly fighting with itself, causing bafflement, fatigue, tension and self-loathing.

In Buddhism, we call this kind of mental behaviour a *saṅkhāra* which means habitual tendency or volitional tendency. The process is just like learning a foreign language or to play the piano, the more you do something the better you get at it until, one day, you discover doing it has become second nature.

Our demons are deeply entrenched habits of mind. We have been developing our capacity to indulge, destroy, sleep, fret and doubt our way out of problems for years, if not lifetimes. We have in fact become so adept at producing them that we barely even notice ourselves doing it.

Perhaps this is why there is such a strong tradition of personifying unwholesome mental behaviour as a devil that tempts and taunts us from without. We simply cannot believe that anyone would be daft enough to choose to beat themselves up in this way, but choose it we do.

Our demons, like any other life-form, need some kind of sustenance to survive. If it is that they are thriving, reproducing and generally taking over then the solution is simple, to stop feeding them. Negative habitual patterns grow stronger on all forms of resistance. Ignore them, suppress them, bully them or hate them all you like, they will just get bigger and nastier.

The desire to manipulate and control what is happening in the mind often stems from a fear that if we do nothing then we will be overrun with undesirable thoughts. This, however, is not so.

The life-blood and oxygen of all defiling states are ignorance and self-concern. We need to cut off their supply by adopting a radically different attitude towards them. This means developing mindfulness in place of ignorance and surrender in the place of self-concern.

The right approach to meditation is to begin with the intention of allowing whatever wants to come into the mind to do so. That really does mean **whatever** wants to come in, without giving in to judgements and comparisons about its relative value. The idea is to remain mindful and self-possessed and to watch with interest what happens, but most definitely not to interfere. Non-interference means to surrender to whatever arises and to restrain the urge to step in and take control of the situation.

Mental events always occur in rapid succession. At first, it is not easy to recognise the links and connections between thoughts. Often in meditation we simply become aware that, at some point, we fell into an unwholesome mental pattern like daydream or worry. How or why we are locked in such thoughts is a mystery at that time.

The trick is to take proper note of the disturbance, to give it an appropriate label, to restrain the urge to indulge such thinking further and to be patient, allowing time for any unpleasant feelings to fade away naturally. As our mindfulness improves it becomes possible to see the links between those kinds of thoughts and the underlying issues that prompted them.

For example, you begin to see that you habitually enter into a daydream as a way to escape from feeling bored. With greater awareness and careful restraint it then becomes possible to stay with that underlying sense of boredom and when you do, you find that feeling bored is not a problem. In fact it starts to fade away even as you watch.

Do you remember those old Tom and Jerry cartoons? The cat, Tom, is frightened by the shadow on the wall of an apparently huge monster heading his way. It turns out, however, that it is a light shining on Jerry struggling round the corner carrying an enormous piece of cheese on his head. Realising this, Tom's attitude changes completely and he rolls up his furry sleeves, grabs the frying pan and starts chasing the mouse around the house all over again.

Defiling states of mind only appear so dangerous or frightening because we do not look at them properly. Once we do they start to shrink in size. The monster reverts to being what it really is, that of a mouse. A hateful thought is just a hateful thought. It cannot overpower you if you label it clearly and watch as it arises, takes hold for a moment only to immediately pass away again.

It takes time, of course, and much by the way of practice. It is inevitable that we will make many mistakes along the way, but if we are willing to persist then gradually, gradually, we begin to master our demons.

Concerning the properly trained mind, Jacqui James (co-founder of the House of Inner Tranquillity) said this: "It's very, very revolutionised, and yet it's still the same. It's just the way you look at it has changed. The way you look at the same old junk... You're not going to get rid of those negative qualities which you find so difficult to handle. What you'll get rid of is finding them difficult to handle."

It is said that when St Anthony emerged after twenty years holed up in a cave in the desert, people were convinced that he would have wasted away and most likely be insane after all that time alone. Instead he emerged healthy and serene.

Seeing the transient and impersonal nature of our inner demons is what frees us from their tyranny. In the end, after much trial and error, you realise that you need do nothing to make them disappear, other than paying proper mindful attention to them without indulging them.

Thus, even as they come and go the mind remains untroubled and as the Buddha states: "Seeing such, that meditator becomes gladdened. This gladness gives rise to delight and the delighted mind generates calm. The meditator who enjoys calmness experiences bliss and being blissful, his mind gains concentration."

Our demons are built from our own deep uncertainties and ignorance about life. You cannot realise *nibbāna* until you have first made friends with your demons. You cannot realise the non-dual while you are still divided and conflicted internally.

It is as if your demons are standing guard at the gateway to enlightenment barring entry and turning you away with promises of illusory pleasures or making you fearful and doubtful.

They are constantly urging you to mistrust and ignore the reality behind appearances, ensuring that you never take that step-less step across the threshold from ignorance to understanding.

It can rightly be said that overcoming your demons **is** the spiritual path. Once you have made friends with them, once you have seen them for what they really are, they can terrorise you no longer and the doorway to peace and contentment is wide open.

Dealing with the Dreamy Mind

A properly concentrated mind is delightful to experience and it well worth the effort involved in learning how to master the skill. Anyone who has tried to meditate, however, knows how challenging it can be. It sounds so simple, to rest content in the moment watching the rise and fall of things. Yet the reality is that this is not such an easy instruction to carry out. There are many different issues that complicate matters but one of the problems common to almost all meditators is sleepiness and the dreamy mind.

This is when you start watching the breathing but within a short space of time find yourself in a dream-like state of mind with a succession of bizarre and random thoughts and images floating across the screen of the mind. Sometimes it can be like entering an entire dream-world. At other times all you are aware of is that for a certain span of time you were not aware of anything. It is like a blank period during which there was no conscious perception and afterwards there is no memory of what happened. It has been known for meditators to occasionally fall so soundly asleep that only the bell at the end of the meditation or their own snoring wakes them up, which can be a bit embarrassing when it happens during a group meditation.

Why does this happen? There are four main reasons:

1. Lack of sleep and general tiredness
2. Meditating after a meal
3. The wilful avoidance of something undesirable
4. Clumsy application

Actually, lack of sleep and general tiredness are not so much reasons as excuses. Often meditators assume that lack of sleep is a bar to successful practice and simply do not even try. This is not, however, the case. With sufficient intent and the raising up of mindfulness, it is perfectly possible to treat tiredness as an object of contemplation. This is done by taking particular interest in its physical and mental characteristics and choosing to observe what happens. Investigation stimulates the mind and taking an interest refreshes it. By letting the whole process occur naturally it is possible to observe how a period of tiredness comes and goes.

Meditating directly after a meal can be a cause of tiredness. This is purely a matter of physiology. The blood supply is being re-directed to the stomach to deal with the digestion of the food and there simply not enough left in the brain to facilitate its optimal functioning. The answer as with general tiredness is to acknowledge the reality of the situation and to wait, mindfully observing and investigating the various sensations in the body. Once the digestive system has completed its task, the blood flow returns to the brain and there occurs a definite and noticeable brightening and lightening of the mental faculty.

Another reason the meditator might become drowsy is as a way of avoiding something undesirable in the meditation. This might be a painful physical feeling or a painful memory or a habitual characteristic that we struggle to accept about ourselves. This wilful avoidance is the hindrance of sloth and torpor. It is the meditative equivalent of turning to alcohol to experience a temporary oblivion from our troubles. Someone who has had a battle with drugs or alcohol in the past will often experience a lot of sloth in meditation.

The only solution here is the systematic setting up of mindfulness with a total willingness to face one's demons and to engage in proper wise reflection to determine what happened and the order of events. Obviously this process is made much trickier by the fact that when you are asleep you have no idea what is going on. With enough intent, persistent application and retrospective analysis, however, you can come to discover what it is that you have been habitually ignoring. Once you know what it is, when it next arises in the meditation you can observe how the mind shuts down and with sufficient practise you can learn how to restrain that particular habit.

And remember, whatever the underlying problem is, its nature is transient and once you see the truth of that you will no longer be troubled by it when it appears.

The fourth reason meditators fall into a dreamy state of mind is through clumsy application. This is concerned with mindfulness and concentration. These two factors of mind are, in fact, especially important in dealing with all the various causes of sleepiness. Much of the problem is caused by not properly understanding that mindfulness and concentration are completely different mental factors and have entirely different functions.

Mindfulness is simply the choice-less awareness of whatever is present in our experience right now, whereas concentration is the focussing of that awareness.

So, for example, in meditation you could have an expanded awareness that took in the perception of your body seated in a chair in the room in which you are located. There may also be awareness of the sounds of birds singing outside and the smell of incense. Compare that to one's awareness being limited just to the area of the abdomen, watching intently the minute movements that occur due to the breathing process but completely oblivious to any peripheral distraction or wider perception. The quality of awareness is the same in each example, what has changed is the size of the area of focus.

The reason meditators fall into daydream is because they attempt to develop their concentration first without having sufficient mindfulness. In essence, they replicate exactly what happens when we go to sleep at night. Without sufficient mindfulness we cannot detect when concentration is giving way to dreaminess and the mind "falls" as it were into the darkness of sleep.

To overcome this tendency the meditator must first recognise the problem for what it is, that of an imbalance of mental factors. The different characteristics and functions of mindfulness and concentration must be properly understood and in all cases mindfulness must be correctly established before attempting to develop concentration.

In practice this means that after sitting down but before beginning to meditate you begin by assessing your general state of mind. With proper awareness established there is the clear comprehension that if you are sleepy then it is not the time to reduce the area of focus to the breath. It is better to keep the mindfulness more general by investigating and noting contacts being presented at the various sense doors. If, on the other hand, the mind is found to be bright and lively, you can begin to reduce the area of focus.

You must, however, use your intelligence and not rush. There is after all the whole period of practice to develop concentration, be it half an hour or an hour. It is better to proceed cautiously, always placing emphasis on mindfulness ahead of deepening concentration.

As the practice unfolds you have to gauge the state of your mind. If it begins to become dream-like, you are advised to bring your attention back to your body sitting in the chair and to move your awareness around to break up the mind and stop consciousness "congealing" into a sleepy state. Once this is achieved you can then try again to focus more exclusively on the breathing.

You cannot do meditation by numbers. To become accomplished you have to learn to adapt your technique to suit the prevailing conditions. It is like sailing a boat, depending on whether the breeze is strong or weak determines how much sail you let out. In all cases of the dreamy, sleepy mind, the resolution is the development of mindfulness, along with intelligent application.

Intent

I smoked like a chimney before I became a monk. Everywhere I went I would carry around a tin of tobacco, replete with papers and a lighter; heavens forbid if I ever mislaid that tin. I inhaled my last roll-up on the public bench on the hill leading up to the monastery just before I entered and it took about two months for the addiction to properly subside. The withdrawal symptoms consisted of relatively mild physical discomfort, but with extreme mental agitation and craving. During such attacks and under the influence of intense longing, I would fantasize about chancing upon a tin of tobacco, just so that I could experience those familiar sensations one last time.

Well, it just so happened that one bright Sunday morning while out for a walk by the river that runs through our town, I noticed something familiar sitting on top of a white fence post. It was an open tobacco tin just like the one I used to carry about and on display right before me was the tobacco, papers and lighter I had been craving. My fantasy had come true.

Was it magic or just a coincidence? Is it possible to create certain outcomes using the power of the mind? Intent is a mental capacity common to all of us. We all use it routinely in our everyday lives and, if properly understood and mastered, it can become a powerful life enhancing tool. The Toltec shamans of ancient Central America conceptualised intent as an impersonal energy that flows through the universe, it could be beckoned through ritual, harnessed, focussed and directed to help them fulfil their goals.

To our modern sensibilities such ideas might appear to be nothing more than superstitious hocus-pocus, but we would do well to pause for a moment and consider our human condition. If we want to do anything, before we can enact it and create an outcome, there must first be the intention to do so. This may seem obvious, but without prior intent nothing would happen. Without intent there would be no St. Paul's Cathedral, no moon landings and Van Gogh could not have painted *The Cafe Terrace at Night* or any of his other wonderful artworks.

Intent is not just required to create the greatest of human achievements, it is also a necessary condition for even the most humble and intimate things we do. We could not stand up, sit down, open a door, say words, or make gestures without the prior intention to do so. What is so special about that? This might appear to be an obvious point, but when you look closely at your personal experience you begin to realise that even the most humdrum activity is actually rather magical.

For instance, without the prior intent, it would be impossible to get out of bed in the morning. Getting out of bed requires the subtle and balanced ongoing co-ordination of hundreds of individual muscles, as well as the brain sending and receiving billions of electrical signals via the nervous system. How does all of that happen so effortlessly? There is an intention to get out of bed, the command is given and, hey presto, you are out of bed. Do you know how it all happens? Are you conscious of and responsible for enacting all those individual movements and activities? If you were, it would probably take you a year just to get out of bed. No, the reality is that all those bodily processes happen by themselves, triggered by nothing more than a simple wish. We really take life for granted, don't we?

Intent is a fundamental and powerful part of our human make-up. What often prevents people from achieving their aspirations in life is a weakness in their intent. If we can learn to consciously harness it, our lives will be that much more satisfying and enjoyable because we will be far more able to accomplish our goals in life. Developing a strong intent is indispensable when it comes to following the Buddha's Noble Eightfold Path.

The training is about facing the reality of your ignorance and overcoming your resistances by learning to surrender to the way life is. Inevitably this means that, from time to time, you will be faced with a real reluctance to practise. After all, learning something new is always uncomfortable and developing enough wisdom to let go of deeply held emotional attachments is very challenging. It is no coincidence, however, that the most worthwhile things in life are always the most difficult to acquire and spiritual enlightenment does not come easily.

So, whether it is leading a more disciplined ethical lifestyle, learning how to meditate, attending classes and retreats, seeking out guidance from real, living teachers or improving one's intellectual grasp of the theory through reading, each and every such activity requires a prior intent if it is to happen at all. And the more you deliberately intend for these things to happen, the more the power of intention is strengthened.

Nothing strengthens intent so much as finding oneself reluctant to do something but then, after suitable reflection, going ahead and doing it anyway.

Recollecting what brought you to the Buddhist path, bringing to mind aspects of the teaching that resonate deeply or recalling what following this way has given you so far in terms of developing understanding and lessening suffering, can all help to rekindle your enthusiasm and commitment.

This includes the times when we need to renounce things as well. My own intent in following this way was helped tremendously by the discovery of that tobacco tin. I could have indulged in a cigarette if that was really what I wanted. I didn't, however, I walked away. What was the point of becoming a Buddhist monk in order to overcome all my attachments to the world if I was just going to surrender to my cravings at the first opportunity? It was nonsensical. I realised that I had created this whole scenario by focusing my extreme longing through fantasy and visualisation. I had created my own problem and right there and then I could renounce acting upon those unhelpful desires and instead increase my intent towards the total cessation of suffering.

Of course, no amount of intention alone can ever possibly produce *nibbāna*. Enlightenment is not a thing to be created. Intention, however, can be used very effectively to develop insight into the transient, unsatisfactory and selfless nature of existence and thereby remove all the ignorance and emotional attachment that prevents the spontaneous realisation from occurring.

So, in that sense, generating positive intentions to develop all aspects of the Buddha's training can be said to be taking us closer to realising the total cessation of suffering. Or, if you prefer, through such spiritual training we beckon *nibbāna* towards us by progressively making ourselves more open and available.

★ ★ ★

As we practise *vipassanā* and investigate our immediate experience, we discover for ourselves the truth that we do create the world around us.

"Mind is the forerunner of all things," the Buddha said. Nothing is solid, everything is in flux and life is fundamentally malleable, mind and matter arise and pass away moment by moment and no moment is ever repeated. There is no predetermination or fate, your future can be altered by your behaviour. It is intention that prompts the arising of *kamma* and is, therefore, intimately bound up with producing future mind and matter. You can and do make things happen using your mind. The more mental clarity, confidence and conscious focusing of the intent, the more clearly defined the result will be.

Here, however, a few words of caution: be careful for what you wish. Using intent consciously does carry risks. One must be clear about one's aspirations and must have a keen sense of right and wrong. It might be harmless enough using visualisation techniques to ensure you find a car-parking space when you go out for the evening or when you pray for someone to get better.

I once, however, met a very successful self-employed man who used focussed visualisations to ensure that he got his own way in business meetings. He wanted to learn concentration meditation and I got the real sense that deep-down what he really wanted was more and more personal power purely for his own advantage. Inevitably, pursuing such power for purely selfish reasons will have a backlash and produce a great deal of pain, anguish and regret, an increase in attachment, an even greater sense of separation, more ignorance, more craving and more suffering.

It doesn't have to be that way. For instance, *mettā* is a Buddhist practice whereby one considers the good qualities of a person and wishes them well. If one wants to learn about and play with intention and visualisation this is a very safe way to do it. Furthermore because it is a relatively selfless and generous activity, it actually yields very favourable results, such as pleasant feelings, clear communications and healthy open relationships, together with a soft, gentle and pliant mind and a greater sense of inclusion in a benevolent universe. When practised correctly and made much of, *mettā* is surprisingly powerful.

A meditator was in Queensland, Australia, driving from Brisbane to Cairns in the north to visit family. He intended to stop off in Townsville on the way to call on a couple of fellow meditators, who had moved to the city from England a couple of years earlier.

He had hoped to contact them before his arrival to let them know he was in the area but discovered that neither of their phone numbers worked. He had their address, however, so after arriving in Townsville and checking into a hotel he went off to find them. He located their house with little trouble but discovered that they were out, so he left a note for them with his contact details and then set off to explore the city.

Whilst out and about he thought it would be a good idea to buy a few supplies for when he continued his journey. He drove around randomly until he found a supermarket, parked up, went inside and down the very first aisle promptly bumped into one of his friends and her two children. The meditator later discovered that, not only did he have the wrong telephone numbers, he had also got the address wrong...

Was it coincidence that they all managed to meet up? Was it magic? Or could it have been the accumulated power of intent?

Uses and Abuses of Mental Energy

To understand the true nature of life requires us to establish a window of awareness in which we can mindfully investigate our immediate personal experience. To create, support and maintain this mental space requires a working understanding of another, generally misunderstood and regularly misapplied mental factor, that of energy. In a list called *The Thirty-Seven Requisites of Enlightenment* energy is mentioned nine times. That is more than any other factor, including mindfulness itself. Energy is the factor of the mind that supports one's chosen endeavour and prevents its collapse, rather like new timbers that help to keep an old house up.

One of the Buddha's monks, the Venerable Sona, wanted to attain liberation and he worked extraordinarily hard, so hard that the path he used for walking meditation was covered in blood from his feet. By his own admission he was one of the Buddha's more energetic students, but despite his supreme efforts enlightenment eluded him. He became depressed and considered giving up and returning to lay life. Before ordaining, Sona had been a musician and was skilled at playing the lute. Knowing this, Gotama guided him using an analogy of tightening strings on a lute: for it to be well-tuned and easy to play, the strings must be neither too taut nor too lax. In the same way, if energy is applied too forcefully in developing mindfulness it leads to pain and restlessness, if it is not applied enough it leads nowhere.

Learning to focus on a single object of contemplation such as the breath teaches us all about the application of mental energy. We discover what is too much, what is too little and eventually experience shows us the optimum level of energy required to keep the mind gently "touching" the object. This is not unique to meditation of course, the artist, the musician, the athlete, the surgeon, they all need to learn about balancing effort as part of perfecting their disciplines. The bee also knows all about balancing energy, reach the flower too early and the pollen is not ready, reach it too late and it has already gone.

The wrong use of energy stems largely from our deep-rooted desire to avoid suffering. For instance, we live in a culture that praises maximum effort and we are taught from a very young age that success and happiness are the result of hard work. So there is a strong tendency towards what in Buddhism we call becoming. In other words we work hard to fulfil a future goal that we ourselves have projected believing that it will give us the happiness we seek.

Conversely, it is also very common to develop a strong aversion to the suffering inherent in hard work and habitually tend towards peace and quiet through inaction and lassitude. There is a flip side to the lazy streak too, whereby we employ maximum effort to get rid of whatever is standing in our way so that we can get back to peace and quiet as quickly as possible.

To a certain extent these techniques must have worked otherwise we would not have employed them so diligently. It is inevitable, therefore, that when we first begin to develop mindfulness we approach the task with the same habitual tendencies. Typically this means that when we begin the training, our application of energy to support mindfulness is extraordinarily heavy-handed. What is actually needed is an exquisite and subtle balance. Put another way, we need to develop a really light touch. Imagine trying to gently keep hold of a little bird in your hand. Squeeze only slightly too hard and you will injure the bird, yet apply too little pressure and the bird escapes.

The Buddha often advised his students to "seize" the object of contemplation with the "eye" of attention. Those who habitually use too much energy try to seize that object with all their might and use all their force in order to subjugate the mind to their will, just as they have in the external world. They are deeply habituated to the idea of a future goal and are used to employing maximum effort. The result of using such force to develop mindfulness is usually crushing headaches, extreme restlessness and agonising bodily tensions.

For the habitually lazy minded individual, "seizing the object" feels like incredibly hard work relative to their normal levels of application. Unwilling to really exert themselves, after a brief flirtation with the task at hand, they soon relapse towards a state of relative inaction and while away their time in daydream and sleep or find a reasonably untroubled mental space to settle down in for the duration.

Inevitably, as happened to the Venerable Sona, when energy is wrongly used, frustration with the practice will grow and grow until a point is reached when one finally accepts the need to adapt one's approach. Sometimes, especially for the over-achiever, the frustration can lead to a spontaneous letting-go of all that striving and, suddenly, in place of the usually cramped, unwieldy and taut mind, there is peace, clarity and spaciousness. At such times meditators often report how simple and effortless it all seems compared with their previous attempts at developing mindfulness. More usually, however, the lesson in how to use the right level of energy has to be learned and relearned many times until it becomes second nature.

With his analogy of the lute, the Buddha is indicating that there is a balance to be struck; a middle way of energy with forcefulness and laziness being the two extremes. To correct the imbalance the meditator needs to adopt the approach of the other extreme. The idea being that in doing so they will pass through the area of optimal energy use and with enough experience will learn to recognise it.

So the energetic worker learns how to restrain the habitual urge to force the pace and, in contrast, the lazybones learns to repeatedly exert firm effort to "seize the object of contemplation" and sustain their application. In practice, it is very difficult to appreciate what the optimal level of energy is compared with our normal, habitual application. This is because the right balance feels so delightfully unhurried, effortless and simple.

For instance, consider the effort that is required to support your intention to read the words on this page. You do not have to try hard at all, do you? And yet there is energy going into preventing your attention from drifting. You can apply the same principle to listening intently to a piece of music or taking in the fragrance of a flower. You require enough energy to simply support your endeavour but do not need to use any unnecessarily excessive force.

It is this very same level of effort that needs to be applied to watching mindfully and noting the arising and passing away of physical and mental events. Compared with its normal habits, however, to the lazy mind this task will appear like an awful lot of hard work and to the overly energetic mind it will seem like being asked to do nothing at all.

In both cases there will be an intense desire to revert to the status quo. After all, these habitual responses are deeply conditioned-in during early childhood and perhaps might even have their roots in past lifetimes. One student reported having visions of her parents standing over her, wagging their fingers at her, telling her she was wasting her time as she sat in meditation learning how to restrain the urge to force results. The ego will use any technique to maintain its dominance.

Managing mental energy effectively requires intelligence. When using energy rightly, it has the delightful feel of working comfortably within one's upper limit. The meditation feels unhurried and the mind is spacious and zestful.

It will not, of course, stay like that for long. Conditions are always changing and so the meditator needs to be flexible enough to adapt the amount of energy used in the course of a session. So if mind or body begin to feel contracted or tight, the meditator learns to ease back and not put in any more volition to be mindful for a little while and wait for the results of the volitions already made to produce their effect. Conversely, if the mind begins to wander, the meditator then uses a little more energy in re-applying focussed attention on the chosen object of contemplation.

At this stage it is a little bit like riding a bicycle. It is not so much about trying to remain in balance as limiting the degree of imbalance by making tiny corrections as you go; now encouragement, now exertion, now restraint.

The key to success in the use of energy is clear comprehension of the overall objective. Freedom from suffering is not some future goal requiring an arduous slog to get there. Freedom from suffering comes from continued mindful investigation of our immediate physical and mental experience. Energy needs to be applied only to the extent necessary to support that endeavour. Whenever one's energy does balance out, the mind becomes spacious, zestful and happy, and practising mindfulness becomes a joy.

Retrospection

Engineers at an aeronautics company designed a window for aeroplane cockpits made from a substance that they believed would be able to withstand the impact of a bird hitting it whilst airborne. Confident of their design, they organised a media event where they would unveil it with a demonstration. To replicate the impact of an aeroplane and a bird colliding in mid-flight, the engineers decided to fire a dead chicken straight at an aeroplane's cockpit window using a high-velocity cannon. Unfortunately, when they shot the chicken at the window, the dead bird not only went straight through the window, it carried on right down the entire length of the fuselage and came out again through the tail.

The engineers were quite taken aback by this unexpected outcome to their demonstration and were at a loss to explain why it had not worked. They went back to the drawing-board and carefully rechecked every element in the design of the window. After six months they felt they were ready for another public demonstration. This time the experiment went exactly to plan. The chicken hit the window but this time bounced off without cracking it. Impressed by this turn round in fortunes, a journalist asked one of the engineers what they had changed from their original design. "Oh nothing," replied the engineer, "It's just that this time we remembered to defrost the chicken."

★ ★ ★

The Buddha maintained that mindfulness is the one way to the cessation of suffering. This is so true. We can never come to the full realisation of enlightenment unless we develop awareness of what is taking place in our experience, moment by moment. Mindfulness alone, however, is not enough. Such presence of mind needs to be supported by another mental quality, that of wise reflection.

The Buddha's son, Rahula, joined the monastic order when still a little boy. One day he was found to have lied. His father gently admonished him. Using the idea of the reflection of a mirror he encouraged his son to contemplate his behaviour in body, speech and mind and whether it harmed him or others or both. If it did, then such an action was not to be performed, if it did not, then it was fine to act in that way.

The Buddha encouraged Rahula to develop this reflective attitude before he acted, whilst he performed an action and subsequent to when he performed an action. Clearly the Buddha was maintaining that everyone, even a little boy, is responsible for their actions and the results that come from them.

Wise reflection is the ability to process retrospectively the information that comes from mindfully investigating our experience. This look back at events is an integral part of developing clear comprehension and wisdom, yet it is an area which is often overlooked, by students and teachers of mindfulness alike.

Where a student is seemingly unable to develop their understanding despite repeated and sustained application to developing mindfulness, the reason is, more often than not, because they have not practised retrospection. The vital information so pains-takingly acquired in the first place is instantly lost again as the mind's ever shifting attention moves on to the next experience. Retrospection gives us the opportunity of a second viewing, a kind of edited highlights show. It is during periods of retrospec-tion that we catch significant events that might otherwise be missed.

Retrospection is about pattern recognition. Wisdom is more than just being aware of our subjective experience, it includes being able to clearly comprehend the order of events and seeing the links and relationships between those events. It is in this way that we come to recognise unmistakably how we create our own suffering.

For instance, a meditator finally comes to understand that the ill-will he directs towards a work colleague is actually an attempt to eliminate the painful feeling he experiences every time he has any contact with her. Further, he sees quite clearly that it is indulging the ill-will that creates the subsequent painful feelings each time they meet. Thus he comprehends that his suffering really is of his own making and has nothing to do with his col-league at all.

In the heat of the moment these links may not be so easy to discern, but in hindsight, when we have calmed down a bit, such patterns can stand out much more clearly.

Retrospection can in fact be developed systematically as part of one's mindfulness practice. At the House of Inner Tranquillity we teach people to break down a period of mindfulness into smaller parts and at the end of each part to incorporate a brief retrospection.

For instance, practising walking meditation around our Japa-nese garden, a student might break up a walk into smaller stages, say, a distance of approximately five metres from the top of the path to the stone lantern and then a similar distance from the lantern to the pond. An intention to stop and reflect at the appointed place is made and then the student gives over completely to being mindful of the physical and mental processes of walking and being aware of and noting any distractions that arise.

Having reached the designated place, the student then stops briefly to see if he or she can remember where the mind went and what happened. Was the student mindful of the changes in motion, pressure, and temperature in the sensations in the soles of the feet? Or was the mind distracted by something? If so, can the student remember what it was and the order of the events?

Having briefly cast the mind back in this way, the student can then let go of any concern about whatever happened, recognising how all those elements have now past away, and set up a new intention for the next stage of the walk.

Another important way to incorporate retrospection is to keep a meditation journal. After each meditation an entry is made of what we can remember happening. The entries do not have to be long neither do they have to be literary masterpieces. The object of the exercise is simply to note down what happened and in what order to the best of one's ability.

Over time, patterns of behaviour begin to emerge and insights into why things occur in the way they do become apparent. The clear comprehension gleaned during periods of retrospection then further supports our meditation practice.

For example, one student often felt a strong frustration whenever she tried hard to restrain the habitual tendency of daydreaming during the meditation. Reviewing the notes in her journal, she observed how regularly this same pattern emerged and it suddenly dawned on her that she was making an assumption.

She had taken it for granted that the frustration was a sign that her efforts to control the mind were not working. Reading her notes she realised that it was actually a sign that she was succeeding and the frustration was simply the mind complaining because it was not being allowed to wander as it had always previously been allowed to do.

This discovery transformed the meditator's attitude and she was able to return to her practice primed and ready to look out for the frustration when it next arose.

★ ★ ★

Often students are willing to set up mindfulness but discover a peculiar resistance to developing the retrospection. Such reluctance may have a variety of causes. Sometimes it is just a lazy approach, whereby the student is unwilling to put in the extra effort required to make it happen. Some meditators on the other hand find it difficult initially to acknowledge negative aspects of their own nature like hatred or conceit. Others may find that they are impatient for results or are mistakenly judging themselves in terms of success or failure based on what their retrospection is revealing. In any event, by not being reflective they can maintain an "ignorance is bliss" attitude.

This is a shame because much of the hard work has already been done. To recognise a lack of mindfulness requires surprisingly good levels of mindfulness. Recognising a negative mental state can easily be regarded as an entirely positive result of practising.

Whilst it can be painful to see that we have not been mindful or discover negative qualities within ourselves, these are, of themselves, not a problem. The problem is self concern, often arising in a form that says: "It should not have been like that" or "I should know better." Believing these thoughts is what often leads students to avoid doing the retrospection altogether.

The remedy is to become mindful of the reluctance when it happens, in order to see for oneself what lies behind it. Is it just laziness or an overwhelming desire to get some tangible results?

Or is it something even more pernicious, like an inability to accept the existence of a negative mental quality like hatred? To find out you must create a strong intention to practise the retrospection with a view to watching the resistance arise. If you can restrain the urge to give in to it and remain alert then it is possible to notice what it is that underlies this non-acceptance.

★ ★ ★

There is another issue with regard to retrospection and this has to do with recognising the difference between wise reflection and speculation. Whereas wise reflection seeks to know only the facts and the order those facts arose in, speculation takes those facts and starts to spin endless webs of hypotheses, possibilities and implications regarding them.

Intellectual types take their own thinking to be the final arbiter or authority of what is right and true. They tend to draw conclusions based on a minimal amount of mindfulness but a great deal of reading, and believe that this is what it is to understand. Such speculation causes doubt in meditators' minds and doubt is a most pernicious hindrance that can destroy all confidence in the practice. At its worst, this approach has even led some to claim to be enlightened when, sadly, anything but this is the reality.

There is a world of difference between practising mindfulness and thinking about practising mindfulness. I estimate that wise reflection and study combined should account for only approximately 20% of a student's overall commitment. The other 80% should be dedicated to direct, mindful experience.

Insights come spontaneously as a consequence of the raw, direct investigation of subjective reality. They are never the product of thought, and the validity of ideas gleaned from study and retrospection need always to be verified through further direct observation.

I remember not long after I had begun my life as a recluse my teacher asked me how I was getting on. After a brief discussion he said that, although it might appear that the Buddha's teaching consisted of a whole bunch of loose ends, with perseverance in the training, the draw strings would finally all come together and I would see how all the various strands actually formed a perfect whole.

He was right, of course, and wise reflection is a fundamental part of that process, helping to connect the theory with the reality of our subjective experience. Whenever such connections are made, that is when the training enters into a whole new dimension in terms of application, enthusiasm and understanding. Then it is as if the whole world lights up before our eyes.

Being Human

Being human is not easy. We are all faced with fundamental life concerns, such as basic survival in a gross physical existence, succeeding in relating socially and pursuing happiness and self-fulfilment, as well as coping with the knowledge of our own mortality. When things do not go well, in addition, we feel the *dukkha* very keenly because we are blessed with very sensitive minds.

Our ability to think is what separates us from the rest of the animal kingdom and we try to co-opt this intellect into finding ways of resolving the problem of suffering. Mostly, however, we humans do not understand the rules that govern how the mind works. We tend to use thinking very inefficiently and our attempts to resolve problems often only exacerbate them. Finding life in some way or other to be unsatisfactory, we can feel very upset and cling to ideas about how it should all be different. Thus, suffering in the form of states such as depression, anxiety and fear remain ubiquitous throughout many people's lives.

For the most part, our modern world believes that it is the duty of science to find ways of overcoming such distressing and unwanted mental states. In the belief that consciousness is entirely the outcome of chemical processes, drugs such as anti-depressants are routinely prescribed for those suffering depression. These have the effect of dulling the mind to any mental pain and anguish that are being experienced.

More recent discoveries in mapping brainwave patterns have led scientists to begin carefully manipulating the brain's chemical functioning in order to "turn off" painful memories, thus giving apparent respite to the sufferer.

While such controls are in force the mind may well appear to be free of suffering. Take away the controls, however, and the problem soon returns with extremely painful results because these chemical solutions merely treat the symptoms of the problem rather than the cause.

Under the blanket of mental fuzziness caused by anti-depressants, the inefficient volitional processes of mind that create and perpetually reinforce the depression are still occurring, multiplying and festering just below the surface level of the conscious mind. In reality, you cannot halt the process of experiencing the results of past action such as painful memories; at best you can only delay them.

Modern psychology is beginning to appreciate more that chemical intervention, whilst providing temporary relief from symptoms, cannot resolve the underlying cause of suffering. Recognising that states like depression are the outcome of mismanagement of the mind rather than chemical imbalance, psychologists are encouraging people to accept responsibility for their own mental behaviour and have embraced the concept of mindfulness or choice-less awareness. Individuals learn to recognise and label the current state of their mind and, having observed what is causing their mental anguish, they can then redirect their energies towards more positive thought processes which produce calmer states of mind.

From the Buddhist perspective, this new approach of mindfulness based cognitive behavioural therapy (CBT) is a welcome development. It is based on a more accurate assessment of the real causes of suffering, that of personal, volitional mental behaviour, rather than merely blaming it on chemical imbalance and relying on medical intervention.

Buddhists, however, would also argue that in using only certain parts of the Buddha's training, modern psychology is ignoring other critically important aspects of how mind and body work. It is essential to understand these in order to completely overcome states like depression.

As it stands modern psychology's use of mindfulness only goes as far as controlling inefficient mental behaviour. Not unsurprisingly, it lacks the understanding of how these states can be eradicated forever. It does not have the vision of the Buddha's enlightened mind.

Mindfulness is an essential cornerstone of the Buddhist way, but it is just one factor in a comprehensive strategy for overcoming suffering. For instance, in addition to mindfulness you do need to get your views right about how life works, which includes understanding rebirth and *kamma*. There is as well a requirement for a comprehensive insight into transience and conditionality.

Whilst one would not generally expect, or indeed require, branches of learning such as medicine or psychology to endorse such ideas, if someone undertakes mindfulness training without these additional components, then the suffering can never be entirely eradicated.

We all appear on this earth from previous existences with the roots of all our positive and negative tendencies firmly established. These come with an infinite store of past actions that only require the presence of suitable supporting conditions to start producing their effects. Given that these basic characteristics include inefficient mental behaviour such as greed, hatred and delusion and are common to all human beings, it means that unhappy external circumstances such as war, terrorism, economic meltdown and man-made environmental catastrophe are inevitable.

The same inevitably applies with the unwanted circumstances of our personal lives, such as the break-up of relationships, financial uncertainty and physical ailments. Even the circumstances of our birth and the subsequent early-life experiences we go through are not random. They are "chosen" for us by our own past action and it is no coincidence that they exert a powerful influence on the way our lives develop from then on.

From the Buddhist point of view, with its mix of painful and pleasant experiences, our brief visit to this human realm can be regarded as the ideal opportunity to learn lessons about how life really works.

We are here to learn about what being a human actually feels like, including all the good bits and all the bad bits. Our mindfulness, therefore, is aimed at including and accepting the whole spectrum of possible physical and mental experiences and our responses to them.

This is why incorporating mundane right view is entirely germane to successfully developing mindfulness. To practise mindfulness requires us to accept the totality of our human condition and to learn to stop resisting the truth of what we find. After all, that is what choice-less awareness means.

Many people's psychological stumbling blocks revolve around being unable to accept aspects of their own nature that they are conditioned to believe should not be there. These may be states of mind such as anger, depression or lust, they may be painful memories of past events or they may be perceived personal shortcomings and failings. They could even be good qualities they refuse to acknowledge.

The prevailing secular notion is that these are abnormal oc-currences and, because of the strong tendency to identify them as being part of the "self," this means that we mistakenly conclude that we ourselves are abnormal. When we use drugs or when we seek psychiatric intervention of one sort or another including CBT based mindfulness, we are seeking normalisation. That is also what the medical professionals seek, they wish to bring us back to what everyone assumes is "normal."

Whilst recognising that for society to function adequately its members need to act within a broad spectrum of accept-able behaviour, in Buddhism there is no such thing as normal or abnormal, there is only that which is. If there is anger in the mind, that is the reality of that moment, it could not be different. If you were told as a child by your parents that you were no good and this conditioning is what now stops you from accomplishing your goals in life, then that is the reality, it could not be different. These situations do not make you abnormal, quite the reverse, these things are normal for a human being to encounter. That is what being human is like.

Understanding the reality of condition dependent origination* eliminates the need to find some first cause for distressing pat-terns of mind. All that is necessary to overcome the problem is choice-less awareness of the pattern as it arises now. It works like this.

In the past, given a certain situation, you responded in a cer-tain way to try and make things different. Given a similar situa-tion now, a similar kind of response arises. Such action now will give rise to similar results in the future and, without sufficient mindfulness, your conditioning will cause you to blindly react in a similar way yet again.

It is an endless cyclical process of the same pattern. Trying to unlock depression or anxiety through finding a first beginning

---

*see appendix I page 187

in this lifetime is short-sighted, ultimately futile and actually counter-productive. It tends to reinforce belief in the narrative of "me" feeling "abnormal" because of "my problem" and, therefore, strengthens resistance and clinging attachment.

The solution, and the secret to mindfulness, is not to seek a solution. It is what one Buddhist teacher calls "the wisdom of no escape." We do not practise mindfulness to eliminate unwanted mental states. We practise mindfulness in order to look at and understand all mental states. Wisdom is the product of observation not intervention.

The great fear, however, for most people is that if you do nothing then this depression or anxiety and the painful feelings that come with them will remain and you will be left feeling abnormal forever. This, however, is not true. It is a delusion that misperceives life and constantly misinforms us. States of depression do not last and the painful feelings do not last. They arise and pass away due to conditions, for that is their nature.

With Buddhist mindfulness practice, the over-arching aim is to see the three marks of all conditioned things, those of transience, unsatisfactoriness and non-self, in all component parts of conscious experience. That is why it is so important to be completely open to the totality of what it is to be human. It is the insight-wisdom gained that ultimately eliminates states like depression, because the roots of all such mental behaviour are based in ignoring reality and craving for it to be different. When you stop resisting and look directly at the transient, ungraspable and selfless nature of reality, you stop suffering.

Seen in this light, one must question the use of anti-depressants by serious Buddhist practitioners because such interventions deepen the tendency to ignore the transient and conditioned nature of the very states of mind that need to be observed.

It goes without saying, of course, that if someone is in the grip of an intense depression or psychotic episode, then out of concern for their immediate health and well-being, it is only right and proper to accept the help of medical professionals. If, however, a meditator is routinely using such drugs long-term they need to consider a staged withdrawal (again, under the supervision of a medical professional) alongside the development of some form of mindfulness and cognitive behavioural therapy. Over time the mind will become calm enough and the mindfulness keen enough to let go of the dependency and then developing insight-wisdom becomes possible.

Incidentally, CBT is nothing new. Such techniques are already to be found within the Buddha's dispensation. Practising the formal recollections of the *Buddha*, *Dhamma* and *Saṅgha*, recollecting peace, practising gratitude, reflecting on one's good fortune or developing the meditations on loving-kindness, compassion, sympathetic joy and equanimity are all forms of what today we call cognitive behavioural therapy. They are all thought processes that take very positive objects of contemplation and all have the effect of pacifying the troubled mind. Replacing the bad with the good is "Right effort" in the Noble Eightfold Path.

Ultimately, through mindfulness we discover that life as it is right now is beyond both good and bad and, in reality, you are something far beyond labels such as "normal" and "abnormal." Stay with and observe those states you habitually resist and ignore, and you will see for yourself that there is nothing whatsoever you need to do to resolve the problem. Yes, it will feel uncomfortable at first but the more you intend to simply stay where you are, looking deeply into the true nature of whatever is present, the less those states will obsess and overrun you.

Cosmic Joke

Some spiritual teachers contend that there is no path or way to enlightenment and that to follow any kind of system of mental development is merely to carry on actively ignoring reality. This, they say, is because truth, understanding, call it what you will, is not the outcome of anything that you do. Rather, it is only when you spontaneously give up all searching, or improvement or manipulation of life, that the recognition of the timeless can occur. The assertion is merited and yet at the same time is somewhat misleading.

With enlightenment comes the complete comprehension that, in one sense, there was never a need to follow a spiritual path. You realise that, since beginning-less time, you had been searching for something that was always present. It was never denied to you, you simply ignored it. Like looking for your glasses and then, after a frantic search, realising that you were wearing them the whole time. And this is the great cosmic joke, that there is actually no need to undertake the journey to freedom because, in reality, you are already free.

To really discover the truth of this for yourself, however, requires that you follow your own personal spiritual journey all the way to its very end. For how can there be an end of all seeking without thoroughly searching in the first place? The suggestion that there is nothing that you need do is only really helpful to someone who has genuinely come to the end of the spiritual training, is free of all attachment, but not yet fully enlightened. Such an individual is said to be at the "gateway" to full enlightenment, which is a very perplexing place. Giving him or her one last riddle to chew on is entirely appropriate and necessary because the question, "Am I enlightened or not?" is the final bastion of ignorance, self-deception and attachment. Other than with this notable exception, however, giving people the idea that there is nothing you need to do is disingenuous and very much to the seeker's detriment.

What a student must hold in mind is that the Buddha never intended his Noble Eightfold Path to bring about full enlightenment. What following this path does, and does supremely effectively, is to remove all the obstacles that *prevent* total understanding from arising.

These obstacles are the things we believe we depend upon for our happiness and with which we identify. They are our deeply held emotional attachments, and to keep them in place requires us to ignore continually the true nature of reality.

The removal of all existential crutches is the purpose of *vipassanā*, which is the meditation on transience that generates delusion-busting insight-wisdom. Only once all the obstacles have been removed can full enlightenment happen, and then only in its own time and own way. It never comes according to your wishes or through any endeavour on your part. True enlightenment is entirely unpremeditated and spontaneous.

If your approach to *vipassanā* is correct, then you are not actually searching for anything at all during meditation. Rather, you are content to note whatever arises naturally in your subjective experience at any given moment. You are not seeking for anything, not even insights, but you allow the reality of transience to impact fully upon your mind and simply wait. After all, it is ridiculous to suppose that you could know what an insight is going to be before it happens. The whole idea of *vipassanā* is to see things never seen before.

Were we to add up the time it takes to go through all the various insights that arise in the course of practising *vipassanā*, without including the gaps between them, it would probably all be done and dusted in under a minute. What takes the time is training a mind that is utterly habituated to avoiding suffering at all costs to stop doing that and instead pay exquisite mindful attention to transience. Anyone who has ever sat down to meditate knows how difficult this is in practice. Craving for life to be different conditions really deep-rooted habitual behaviours and we will not surrender them lightly.

Imagine a scene where you are standing on a path with your spiritual guide who is directing you to a gate a short distance away. "Go through that gate and be free," she says. You look around and see lots of other students all of whom apparently want to go through that gate too yet seem to be doing anything but that. One person is fast asleep in a deck chair, another is compulsively sweeping the path with a broom, while someone else is walking around with their eyes closed bumping into everything. One person sits happily writing a really nice poem about the gate, while in a near-by field someone else is frantically running about in circles. You see one chap lying on the ground prostrating in front of the gate and a lady stood rock-solid with arms crossed against her chest angrily berating the teacher and shouting, "There are no paths, there is no way, there is nothing you need do!" To each and every one the teacher continues to point and say, "Go through that gate and be free."

It is entirely understandable that people will adopt the same habitual avoidance techniques and displacement activities on the spiritual path that they use in the rest of their lives. That is why the three trainings, in ethics, mental control and wisdom, are so indispensable. They teach us *how* to let go of these inefficient responses.

One wonders how it is possible to realise enlightenment without such discipline. Students sometimes ask me if there is a short-cut to enlightenment to which I respond, "The Buddha's teaching is the short-cut." In point of fact, it is more accurate to state that there really are no short-cuts, but that the Buddha's training represents one very direct route to non-suffering. How short and speedy that journey is depends on the individual, the nature and strength of their attachments and their level of maturity in relating to the teacher and the training.

Letting go of all deep-rooted emotional attachments is the necessary prerequisite for the realisation of enlightenment, irrespective of who you are, where you come from and what you know. Whilst you still believe that there are things to identify with and that they can be depended upon for happiness, you will carry on depending on them. Whilst there remains even the merest sliver of attachment to anything, anywhere in time, space and consciousness, then you are tied forever to suffering. Only once all such attachment has been surrendered through seeing perfectly that there is nothing to own, control or grasp, can the reality that lies beyond time, space and consciousness be laid bare.

The Buddha's training is designed to teach us how to stop acting upon the urge to avoid the truth of suffering and how to look reality squarely in the face. It is designed to straighten out and shorten our skew-whiff journey. It shows us how to develop the capacity for mindful, unbiased observation of subjective experience, to generate the wisdom that eliminates the craving for life to be different. The gateway to enlightenment is what remains once that has been accomplished. It is always available, ready and waiting to be discovered.

The beautiful paradox is that, once finally through the gate, you look round and discover that, in reality, there never was a gate there at all and no path and no teacher, and no time has elapsed or ever could elapse. All there has ever been is timeless perfection. So you finally come to understand the great cosmic joke, that there really was nothing you had to do at all.

Or was there?

The Building Blocks of Experience

The purpose of *vipassanā* meditation is to clearly comprehend the difference between the way things appear to be, as solid, separate and enduring, and the deeper reality wherein the things of the world are understood to be empty, transitory and illusory.

To see life as it really is first requires us to abandon our emotional dependency on the things of the world. While we are still in the thrall of our attachments we will continue to have a vested interest in wilfully ignoring and misperceiving reality. Letting go of attachments can only be achieved by training ourselves to observe closely the moment by moment flow of conscious experience. In this way we can correct the hallucinations of perception that cause us to mistake what is actually there with what is presumed to be there.

It is a sign of how deeply mired the average person is in hallucination, that when being exposed to these ideas for the first time most find it all rather baffling. After all, it is obvious that there is a world full of separate things, isn't it? I mean, just look around you.

What follows is an explanation of how it is that your perception of life really does deceive you. It cannot be stressed enough, however, that while explanations are useful, in the end it is only through experiencing these things directly that true understanding comes.

The first thing we need to consider is that Buddhism offers two distinct but interconnecting ways of interpreting life, those of conventional reality and ultimate reality. For each level there is a description of what elements exist within it and how those elements relate to one another. Rather like Newtonian physics and quantum physics, there are unique laws that govern each level that do not pertain to the other. In other words, you cannot describe one level of reality using the rules and language intended for the other.

Conventional reality, as the name suggests, is the description of life with which we are already familiar. It is the world of discreet, separate objects, of you and me, of trees and flowers, of places and events, of days, weeks, months and years, and of stars, planets and moons. The Buddha's teaching offers a comprehensive set of guidelines on how to get the most from living in this world. It teaches us the basic laws of conventional life, such as how our actions have results and how life goes on in an endless succession of rebirths.

Ultimate reality is different. Here the description is of the fundamental building-blocks that go to make up subjective experience, and the laws that govern how in an endless stream they come into being and pass away again due to conditions. Herein we do not find a "you" or "me" or "flower" or "yesterday." For instance, in ultimate terms there is no-one who sees. There is, however, the sensitive matter of the physical eye that reacts to light waves falling upon it and which is the base upon which seeing consciousness arises as a consequence. Again, there is no "thinker" but there most definitely is mind, which is the base upon which thoughts, feelings, perceptions and other mental activities arise.

During *vipassanā* meditation, the whole of subjective experience is intuitively broken down into its constituent parts and the behaviour of those parts and their relationship to one another is investigated. The way in which these impersonal building-blocks of mind and matter arise and pass away, link, combine and weave together to create the appearance of a world of solid, enduring objects is comprehended. It is this insight-wisdom that destroys the hallucinations of perception that give rise to all possible emotional attachment to the world.

Finally, in the absence of any emotional dependency upon any "thing" whatsoever, there is then nothing to prevent the full comprehension of that which lies beyond this endless weaving together of experience.

★ ★ ★

To help us define an otherwise amorphous mass, the Buddha divided ultimate reality into five distinct groups called *khandha* or aggregates. These are materiality, feeling, perception, mental formations and consciousness.* They represent all aspects of mind and matter both internally and externally.

It is out of these five aggregates that the illusory worldly things with which we identify and form emotional attachments are woven, and nothing we experience could possibly be found outside of these groups. The *vipassanā* technique is to be mindful of our actual moment to moment experience and to note the arising of any of these five aggregates.

By way of an example and to underscore the point that this process is not restricted to sitting meditation, let's pay close attention to what is happening at the ultimate level when engaged in the simple act of smelling a rose and resolve some of the elements at play down into the five *khandha*.

---

*see appendix II page 189

1) The aggregate of Materiality consists of all ultimately existing physical phenomena. In the experience of smelling a rose, things that could be noted would include the shape and colour of the visible object and the eye-base being the sensitive matter that senses the object. There is also the smell of the object and the nose-base being the sensitive matter that registers the smell. There is lastly the pressure, temperature or motion in the sense of touch and the body-base being the sensitive matter that senses them.

2) The aggregate of Feeling consists of that aspect of mind which experiences the "flavour" of the object, which can be noted as being pleasant, unpleasant or neutral. In the instance of smelling the rose's fragrance, the feeling of pleasure is noted. Upon catching one's finger on a thorn, an unpleasant feeling is noted.

3) The aggregate of Perception consist of that aspect of mind which applies a label to an object. If upon visual contact with the object recognition of plant, rose, climber or Dundee Rambler arises in the mind, then the label of perception is applied.

4) The aggregate of Mental Formations is wide-ranging and consists of all aspects of mind other than feeling, perception and consciousness. For instance, some of the mental formations involved in the experience of smelling the rose would be: attention, one-pointedness, contact, pleasurable interest, desire-to-do, intention, volition, and investigation; to name but a few.

5) The aggregate of Consciousness consists of that aspect of mind which "knows" the object. If it is a visual object then seeing or eye-consciousness is noted, if it is a smell then smelling or nose-consciousness is noted and so on.

We could continue but that gives us the general picture. By observing and noting in this way we find that within the experience of "smelling a rose" there is a complex array of different mental and material factors at work. Each does an individual task in creating the overall event, but there is nothing concrete and solid that, in and of itself, constitutes a "rose" or "me" who smells.

In every experience looked at in this way we find that the underlying pattern is the same. There is nothing static or enduring in any of it and nothing stands alone. Every individual element is found to be utterly fleeting and is entirely dependent upon other, equally transient elements for its momentary existence.

From continued observation we eventually reach a point where we see directly for ourselves how it is that the apparent reality of "smelling a rose" is actually a complex weaving together of the building blocks of ultimate experience and, when you get right down to it, the whole experience is empty of any intrinsic reality. It is a *conceptual* interpretation of reality rather than what is *actually* experienced.

To crave and cling to any experience in the belief that it will bring genuine happiness requires the continued misperception of life as enduring, satisfactory and ultimately controllable, and this means continuing to ignore the deeper reality. Consciously turning the mind to look at the building blocks of any experience and repeatedly noting the transient, ungraspable and conditioned nature of whatever arises, naturally begins to undermine those misperceptions and, therefore, craving and clinging attachment.

So, what difference does the direct comprehension of the ultimate nature of reality make? Life carries on in much the same way as it always has, but is now free of any emotional dependency upon any part of it. Just as you know when you sit down to watch a soap opera on television that none of it is really real and yet you are still able to partake in the story and even empathise with the plight of the characters, so, in the same way, you realise what a wonderful "cosmic soap opera" life really is. It is indeed empty of any intrinsic reality and yet there is something there and what is there is endlessly new, fascinating, wonderful and mysterious. Through the generation of insight-wisdom you teased life apart, then put it back together again and now you know what is real and what is merely conceptual. As the Buddha declared, "I use the terms, but I am not confused by them."

Only once you have fully comprehended how the world is magically woven together moment by moment from these fleeting building blocks of experience, only then do you realise what perfection really is and truly understand what it means to be free.

Beyond Time and Space

One of my students gave me a card for my birthday. On the front was a cartoon of a chicken having an argument with an egg and the egg is shrugging and saying, "Well, let's not worry about it. All that matters is that we are both here now."

There are lots of theories concerning the first beginnings of things. It is a hot topic. Many people seem to think that it is through understanding our origins that we can solve the whole mystery of our existence and, therefore, our suffering.

At the beginning of his book *A Brief History of Time*, the renowned theoretical physicist Stephen Hawking tells the creation story of the Boshongo people of central Africa. They believe that before us there was only darkness, water and the great god Bumba. One day Bumba, in pain from a stomach ache, vomited up the sun. The sun evaporated some of the water, leaving land. Still in discomfort, Bumba vomited up the moon, the stars and then the leopard, the crocodile, the turtle and finally, humans.

Whether we argue that time and space all began with a super high-powered tiny dot spontaneously exploding, or with a deity troubled by wind, neither view actually resolves the mystery of our existence. As we all know, for every effect there is always a prior cause. From where did Bumba and his grumbling tummy appear? And what did cause the Big Bang to occur? Can something arise from nothing or is there only infinite regression? Where do things begin and where do they end? Could there ever be such a thing as a causeless cause?

People talk about creation myths, but could it be that the very notion of first beginnings is the real myth? Could it be that there never was a universe, as we normally understand it to be, that exploded into life thirteen billion years ago. Perhaps what does ultimately exist, the ever changing flow of conscious experience, is a process occurring outside the constraints of time altogether.

To most people, the perception of an indubitably real universe is so strong that any talk of it being otherwise is likely to be dismissed out of hand. Sometimes, however, you have to be prepared to take a risk, to "think outside the box" and find a way to circumvent the limitations of conventional thought and fixed perceptions.

So, as a little thought experiment, let's consider this: why do we always assume that existence flows in a straight line? Why couldn't it be spherical instead? Imagine an ant crawling on the surface of an orange suspended in space. No matter how long and hard he travels neither the orange's beginning or end will be discerned by that ant. The nature of the orange isn't the problem, it is the ant's limited view of things that is the problem. So it is with existence itself. Only if it is assumed to be linear like a piece of string are we forced to consider beginnings and endings and causeless causes.

The Buddha stated that one cannot reach the end of the world through travel. What did he mean? In the Buddhist view of life, the world of duality, *saṃsāra*, is a beginning-less, endless cycling of conscious experience and no amount of travel through either time or space will ever bring you to the end of it.

For, at the epicentre, keeping the wheel in perpetual motion is simple cause and effect, the law of *kamma*. This law states that all self-conscious volitional activity must produce results and those results are to be consciously experienced as the feelings and perceptions that arise due to sense-contacts.

It is to experience the results of past action that the present mind/body complex exists, within an environment that offers suitable life-support and with which it interacts. That being the case, there now arises an endless stream of sensory contacts, feelings and perceptions. Some are agreeable and much sought after, others are unpleasant and unwanted. It is in response to this constant flow of resultants that new self-conscious volitional activity is performed, constantly seeking out the desirable and trying to avoid the undesirable. It is these fresh desires for yet more sensory experience and renewed existence that will necessitate the production of future mind and body.

So each moment in the stream of conscious experience has both active and passive phases, causes and effects. Each action will condition another result and each result will condition another action. This same fundamental pattern, which in Buddhism is called condition-dependent origination or *paṭicca-samuppāda*, is repeating at all levels of existence. It occurs within each moment, throughout the course of a lifetime and with each subsequent rebirth. This is why no action can ever get you off the wheel of becoming, because it is the very actions you perform that propels the cycle. And so it goes on and on, and round and round, and round again.

Here we can see the stark difference between the Buddha's description of the world and the scientific theory of materialism that is so in vogue at the moment. Science contends that the universe is fundamentally physical in nature and that the arising of consciousness is an epiphenomenon, the accidental outcome of the coming together of material processes. It is undeniably the case that material processes are involved in the production of conscious experience and to this degree Buddhism is in agreement with science.

Gotama further understood, however, that the arising of the material processes that help enable consciousness to occur, do so as a result of prior craving. Looked at this way the universe appears very different indeed. Rather than being an outcome of chance, everything in the material universe, from the smallest atom to the largest star, is actually part of the process that allows resultant conscious experience to emerge. To this end the "creator" of this vast, infinite, dualistic universe is simply the prior volitional desire for it. As the Buddha stated so emphatically, "Mind is the forerunner of all things." This includes even time, space and matter. That is why the Buddha would never answer questions about the first beginnings of things as such questions could only be formulated based on a false first premise.

★ ★ ★

The truly timeless nature of existence really becomes obvious when we practise *vipassanā*. We focus our attention on the transient and conditioned nature of all sensory events. Doing so, we become increasingly aware that any moment of conscious experience arises and passes away again instantaneously and that there is absolutely no remainder. That is to say, nothing whatsoever is found that persists from the past through to the present and into the future. Not consciousness, not the object of consciousness, not the media of sense, not the perception of the object, not the feeling that arises nor the volitional response to that feeling. As our discernment deepens and the insights keep coming, we comprehend that the entirety of subjective experience comes into being now and ceases now. It is woven together by an infinite array of impersonal conditioning forces acting upon one another, only instantly to dissolve again.

Insight-wisdom drives a wedge of understanding between the world as conceptualised by thought versus the world as actually experienced. Only in the conceptualised version is there a past, present and future. In actuality there is only the moment, this moment, now, which is not time-bound.

For the practising *vipassanā* meditator the Big Bang did not happen thirteen billion years ago. If there is a "Big Bang" at all, it is happening right now.

The enlightened mind intuitively understands the illusory nature of existence. Notions of time and space are founded on comparison and the relativity between "things." They, therefore, only pertain where there is dualistic consciousness, i.e. the assumption of "self" and "other." In the absence of dualistic consciousness there is only "that which is," the non-dual, without centre or circumference. That understanding is not in itself subject to the vagaries of passing time. It is not a "thing" that exists in relation to other "things." It does not come and go. It is totally beyond time and space.

All questions about the beginning and ending of the universe dissolve in the light of this understanding. Understanding gleaned, not from speculation, conjecture, or supposition, but from the simple unbiased observation of reality as it really is.

It is not that you are trapped by time, you are beyond time. You are trapped only by the assumption of your own separateness. This takes as absolute truths the concepts of "self" and "universe" and gives rise to all the emotional attachments that are subsequently formed because of that division.

Enlightenment is to surrender everything to the wonder and the mystery of existence. There is a total and joyous surrender to the infinite unknown. You hold on to nothing, seek for nothing and retain nothing.

Freed from the limiting, repetitive and unsatisfactory cycles of *saṃsāra*, you find that to dwell in the great timeless mystery is all you ever wanted. In fact, you realise it is all that there has ever been, temporarily covered over by ignorance, but now blazing with the brilliance of a million stars.

What is Consciousness?

Someone I know is a very deep sleeper. One morning in 1987 he woke up to discover that most of the trees in his garden, along his street and down the main road had been thoroughly uprooted during the night. There had been a great storm with hurricane-force winds that had lasted three or four consecutive hours during the night. He had somehow managed to completely sleep through it all, he hadn't heard a thing.

There is so much uncertainty and speculation around the subject of consciousness, which is remarkable considering how utterly familiar we all are with it. What is consciousness? It is that which constitutes the knowing or awareness of an object. It is experiencing the pain of a headache, the tasting of wine or seeing a golden sunset. This is what it means to be conscious.

Yet, for some reason, we feel compelled to turn to the "experts," the scientists, the philosophers and the psychologists, to explain it all to us. And what a complex and unwieldy affair their theories and speculations turn the simple act of awareness into.

It is entirely possible to come to a complete understanding of consciousness, not through thinking about it or trying to measure it, but through the simple, clear and direct observation of it as it occurs. Through such observation we can fully comprehend not only what consciousness is but also, and perhaps even more importantly, what it is not.

Why is understanding consciousness so important? The Buddha included consciousness as one of the five aggregates, which along with feeling, perception, mental formations and materiality, make up the whole of subjective experience at the ultimate level. Due to ignorance we cling mightily to the deeply-held emotional conviction that these five aggregations are facets of a solid and separate entity, ego or personality, i.e. "me." We whole-heartedly believe, therefore, that it is "me" that knows; it is "me" that sees, hears, smells, tastes and touches. It is "me" who is the conscious witness to all of life's events, distinct and entirely separate from the sights, sounds, smells, tastes and touches of the external world. We believe this dualism to be so and perceive it to be so. To such an extent indeed that we never stop, even for a moment, to ask ourselves whether it is at all possible or even necessary for consciousness to have an owner or whether that sense of separateness relates to anything real.

If there really is a separation, however, between an experience and "me" who experiences it, between consciousness of an object and the object itself, then it should be possible to locate that exact line.

As an experiment, observe a distant visible object like the disk of the moon and ask yourself, "Where do I stop and where does the moon begin? Where is that line of separation?" This is not an intellectual exercise, don't think about it, just observe your experience. Where does that line occur which differentiates direct awareness of a thing from the thing itself? Does it even exist?

Gaining insight into the true nature of consciousness is fundamental to realising enlightenment and it pays to keep things as simple as possible.

Throw out all those tangled theories about what you or others think consciousness is and practise mindfully observing and labelling experience using easily comprehendible information.

For instance there are five physical senses: eye, ear, nose, tongue and body. For each sense there is an equivalent kind of consciousness, i.e. seeing, hearing, smelling, tasting and touching.

For ease of exposition, the Buddha talked of mind as being the sixth sense so there is also mind-consciousness, i.e. the awareness of mental activities such as thoughts, feelings, perceptions, memories, fantasies and the like.

In addition there is one more type of consciousness called mind-consciousness-element which will be discussed later. That makes a maximum of seven distinct "kinds" of consciousness that can be observed and labelled.

The art of *vipassanā* is simply to investigate one's immediate experience and mentally note whatever occurs. If the sound of an ambulance siren occurs then "sound" is noted and also the "perception" of the ambulance.

As insight develops it becomes possible to differentiate consciousness from the object. It becomes obvious, for instance, that sound is one thing and hearing, the knowing of sound, is another. The same applies to awareness of mind states with perception being one thing and the awareness of that perception, mind-consciousness, being another.

As noting continues and insight deepens it gradually becomes clear that, despite being two entirely dissimilar things, any sensory object and its equivalent consciousness arise in unison and that you cannot have one without the other.

If there is no sound, no hearing arises, if there are no thoughts or other mental objects, such as when in deep sleep, no mind-consciousness arises. Equally, if there is no hearing, literally no sound exists, as in the example of the man sleeping through the storm.

Thus, the reality of conditionality becomes clear at a very intimate level for the meditator. Consciousness and object are mutually dependent upon one another for their existence, you cannot separate them.

It also becomes self-evident that neither consciousness nor its object last for more than the briefest of moments. As quickly as they come into being, so they pass away again. One moment of consciousness must immediately cease in order to allow another moment of consciousness to arise.

Look closely and you discover that consciousness arises in series, you can never be aware of more than one object at a time. If seeing-consciousness arises then that is all that exists at that moment, there is no hearing, smelling, tasting, touching or mind-consciousness. Given their interdependent natures it is obvious that if either consciousness or its object is removed, in that instant, the other also ceases.

So we discover that there is no permanent, unchanging and ongoing consciousness that can be identified and grasped after as being "me" or "mine."

What we do find, however, is an endless stream of momentary occurrences of consciousness that arise and pass away in a completely natural and spontaneous way. Just like a river, the bubbling stream of conscious experience has no discernible first beginning. It flows on endlessly in an entirely impersonal way and is never the same for two consecutive moments.

The meditator comprehends that all awareness of whatever kind is wholly and forever *anattā*, non-self. It cannot be underestimated what a seismic shift in your perception of life this discovery brings.

Who or what, however, is it that knows all this? Surely "I am" the permanent conscious witness behind this ceaseless flow of sensory events, the one who knows that consciousness is non-self?

When, inevitably, this question arises for a meditator they are directed right back to watching the arising of consciousness with two questions: does the awareness of any of the six other types of consciousness last, and if none of the six types of consciousness arise can any subsequent awareness of them arise? Through direct insight into the matter the meditator is able to give a definitive answer, "No," on both counts.

In Buddhism, the awareness that takes the immediately preceding moment of consciousness as its object is called mind-consciousness-element. It too arises entirely due to conditions and passes away immediately. It is this seventh type of consciousness that people often mistakenly assume is the "self" or conscious witness existing behind or parallel to events.

Mind-consciousness-element is subtle and without paying proper attention it is easy to misperceive it as being permanent and unchanging. Look closely, however, and you will see that, just as with every other kind of consciousness, it can only arise dependent upon a suitable object being present and ceases immediately.

Through insight the understanding comes that there is no durable, independent witness behind events at all.

★ ★ ★

Some people mistakenly associate consciousness with *nibbāna*. During meditation, when the mind is calm and free of hindrances, it is possible to perceive geometric space as extending out in all directions to infinity. It is then easy to conceptualise how all imaginable physical and mental objects might enter into, inhabit and exit this plane of infinite space.

Concluding that consciousness of this plane of infinite space must also be infinite, there is a strong urge to assume that infinite consciousness is the answer. This assumption, however, is wrong and ignores so much.

Consciousness can take anything as an object including such subtle and vaunted states as the plane of infinite space. No matter how impressive the object is, however, the fundamental nature of awareness is to arise due to conditions and immediately pass away. The fact that this particular consciousness takes infinity as its object does not make it eternal.

The hallucination of permanence, however, causes the meditator to conceptualise this infinite space as being ongoing. This is the case even when the mind is engaged in observing something else and, therefore, the meditator believes it is something that endures and can be consciously entered and exited at will. This, however, is not the case.

The meditator ignores the fact that when there is consciousness of one object, no other consciousness or object exists. It may appear that the same object can be held in the stream of consciousness for a protracted period of time, but close observation shows that it is neither the same object nor the same consciousness in successive moments. In reality, each subsequent event is self-similar to the preceding one but never actually the same one.

Nibbāna is beyond consciousness. When you have fully perfected your view and have ceased to misperceive reality, you then understand the true nature of consciousness. You understand that you cannot delineate awareness as a thing in itself distinct from the object of awareness. You understand, therefore, that consciousness divides and that any division creates dissatisfaction, conflict and suffering.

Knowing this you cease to grasp after consciousness as being "self" and in ceasing to grasp, the mind no longer upholds the illusion of dualistic consciousness. All that remains is *nibbāna*.

What is meant by *nibbāna*? It is impossible to define. This beautiful poem, however, by the Tibetan master Nyoshul Khenpo

Rinpoche comes nearer than most in encapsulating its simplicity and wonder:

> "Profound and tranquil, free from complexity,
> Uncompounded luminous clarity,
> Beyond the mind of conceptual ideas;
> This is the depth of the mind of the Victorious Ones.
> In this there is not a thing to be removed,
> Nor anything that needs to be added.
> It is merely the immaculate
> Looking naturally at itself."[*]

---

[*]From elephantjournal.com (12 October 2012) *Quote of the Day: Nyoshul Khen Rinpoche* [Online]. Available from: http://www.elephantjournal.com/2012/10/quote-of-the-day-nyoshul-khen-rinpoche [Accessed 27 October 2014]

A Glimpse of the Beyond

One of the truly astonishing things to happen in the course of following the spiritual way is what in Buddhism we call stream-winning. This is the moment when someone enjoys a first glimpse of *nibbāna*, the beyond.

The Buddha coined the term stream-winning to indicate that people experiencing it are, as a result of this glimpse, assured of realising full enlightenment. They have entered the stream of conscious experience that leads inexorably to the complete cessation of suffering.

The glimpse itself is extremely short-lived. It lasts no more than a finger snap and yet it exerts the greatest possible influence on an individual's life. In that briefest of moments the mind undergoes an extraordinary shift in understanding.

Abandoning its normal preoccupation with the occurrence of things, consciousness has momentarily alighted upon that which neither arises nor passes away. In that moment the mind is no longer perceptually dividing up life between "me" and "not me" or "self" and "other." For the merest flash, there is the complete comprehension that life truly is perfect, and that this is the one true freedom for which everybody seeks.

Not everyone who experiences stream-winning, however, necessarily retains such a commanding appreciation of what has just
happened to them. For the vast majority of those who obtain
this vital glimpse, they do so as part of a formal spiritual training.
Insight meditation, *vipassanā*, is one such training.

In my experience as a *vipassanā* teacher, of those who do realise stream-winning, a few might be clearly conscious of what has
just happened, many will be aware that *something* just happened
but might not be able to put their finger on quite what and
there are a few who genuinely do not seem to have noticed at
all. The difference seems to be in how much concentration the
individual has been able to muster.

It is also possible for such a glimpse to occur for some people
without them being consciously engaged in a particular training,
although this is much rarer. Even in these cases, however, some
past involvement with the spiritual search can be assumed, either
in this life or in lives gone by. Stumbling across a glimpse of the
beyond without any guidance whatsoever is rather like actually
finding the needle in the haystack; not impossible, but highly
improbable.

The moment of the glimpse subsequently gives way to feelings
of euphoria, bliss, sublime happiness and a sense of connection
with a deeper reality. Perceptually the things of the world seem
to have a beauty, an inner shine, that was never noticed before.
This relates not just to objects generally regarded as being beautiful, but even to objects usually dismissed as ugly or uninteresting.
All objects become fascinating and unfamiliar, as if being seen
for the first time.

There is a sense that everything is unified, that there is a nameless quality inherent in and common to all objects, irrespective
of whether those objects are animate or inanimate. It is there
in a stone, in the eyes of your loved ones, in the touch of the
wind against your face and in the flow of people milling in the

town centre. Again, the intensity and duration of such perceptual shifts depend upon how much concentration the individual can muster. Indeed similar states of mind also arise naturally as a consequence of practising concentration meditation.

From this it can be deduced that these various psychological states are not the essential factors in stream-winning, but may be considered to be the graceful adornments that come with it. The intensity of such thoughts and feelings gently recedes over the next few minutes and hours. What is critical is the glimpse of the beyond itself and that is not so much an experience as a realisation.

Whilst the fleeting experiences connected to this first glimpse of *nibbāna* may vary from person to person, the realisation itself is the same for all and leaves certain indelible traits in the mind-stream.

For instance, someone "won to the stream" will have perfect confidence in the *Buddha*, the *Dhamma* and the *Saṅgha*. Now this point needs some clarification. You do not necessarily need to have heard of the Buddha to have that confidence, nor have come across his teaching. The confidence stems from having glimpsed *nibbāna* and therefore knowing from direct, personal experience that there is a beyond. It is not a myth, nor mere superstition, it exists, and it is known that enlightenment is real and attainable. The penny drops that throughout history there have been various great individuals who have not just fully awoken to the truth, but who have also been able to devise genuine ways to show others how to wake up. The Buddha's teaching is definitely not the only way, but it is a very effective one.

As a stream-winner you are also aware of the arising of an absolute inner assurance that you will become fully enlightened. This will be the case even if you are one of those who cannot recall having had the glimpse. This, then, is not about coming to a conscious decision to have faith or drawing that conclusion based on reflecting on events. The sense of certainty in your eventual success is entirely spontaneous, your faith is unshakeable and cannot now be overcome by its opposite, that of doubt. There is no trying to have faith, or deciding to have confidence, it isn't even a conviction. Such assurance radiates from you as naturally as the sun shines.

It goes without saying that all this has a tremendous impact on a person's life and his or her priorities. Quite how profound a change takes place will depend on the individual's personal circumstances at that time. If the person is already firmly established in the teaching, as most are who reach this point, externally life will, likely as not, continue much as before. Where, more rarely, the individual has come upon it without guidance and support, the impact on the person's life may well be greater.

Inwardly, however, a stream-winner is a changed individual. In traditional Buddhism he or she is said to have changed lineage from a worldly person endlessly caught in *saṃsāra* to that of a noble one destined for *nibbāna*. Although most definitely not yet fully enlightened, there are certain negative dispositions which have been eradicated for good and others that have been severely curtailed.

Critically, three psychological fetters, so called because they lash beings tightly to *saṃsāric* existence and perpetuate ignorance and craving, are eradicated forever. These are:

1. The Fetter of Personality Belief. This is the speculative view or assumption that there resides within the processes of the mind/body complex a permanent, unchanging entity or self.

The insight into the egoless nature of reality at stream-winning, however, is not the complete eradication of self-view *per se*. The conceit of selfhood being within the five aggregates does still persist and is only finally overcome through continued insight practice. The assumption, however, of selfhood has been dealt a mortal blow. The first glimpse of *nibbāna* establishes clearly that the physical body is definitely not the self.

2. The Fetter of Sceptical Doubt. As has already been discussed, personal insight into the true nature of reality at stream-winning makes doubting the Buddha or the efficacy of his teaching impossible. Doubt is the most insidious of all the defilements as it is the one that can prevent all spiritual practice. Upon stream-winning faith becomes a power because it can no longer be conquered by doubt.

3. The Fetter of Attachment to Rites and Rituals. You can no longer maintain the belief that freedom from suffering can be gained simply through the performance of certain rituals and ceremonies. This occurs when you see for yourself even for a split second what *nibbāna* is, where it is, and what it was you did or did not do to glimpse it. Deliverance is a matter of understanding.

In addition to the eradication of the fetters, knowledge of the reality of *nibbāna* naturally conditions a virtuous outlook on life. There will be no major transgressions in conduct due to defilements such as envy, hypocrisy, fraud or the denigration of others. The roots of lust, hatred and delusion in addition will have been attenuated enough to prevent heinous crimes such as murder or rape.

The Buddha said that anyone could determine for themselves whether they were a stream-winner by reflecting upon whether they had perfect confidence in the *Buddha, Dhamma* and *Saṅgha,* and moreover, whether they shared in the "Virtues beloved of the Noble Ones."

Stream-winners will naturally live more moderately, and will be much more aware that actions have results. They will tend towards association with others who share these same values and will shy away from those who live entirely without regard for the spiritual life.

The orientation of a person's life changes and the discovery of the permanent cessation from suffering becomes their priority. There is definitely more awareness of the difference between wholesome and unwholesome behaviour after stream-winning, but this, in turn, can create its own problems.

In the immediate afterglow of stream-winning, there is a palpable sense of purity due to a complete absence of defiling states of mind. For a while there is no ignoring and no passionate resistance. Occasionally someone who reaches this point may fall into the trap of believing that this must be full enlightenment.

This is understandable given how serene, blissful and simple life feels, but it is a mistaken conclusion. As time passes these beautiful states of mind begin to recede. As a person reconnects with "ordinary" life and continues to interact with the world, an acute awareness of inefficient habitual responses to events emerges, especially grosser responses rooted in greed and hatred.

It is as if a surface level of ignorance has been swept aside but that this now lays bare the reality of what has always been going on underneath our conscious awareness. We have been so busy acting out of our craving that we have failed to notice what we have been doing, until now. And now it is painfully obvious.

As a stream-winner you are caught in a difficult situation. On the one hand you have discovered what the Buddha referred to as the "eye of *dhamma*," the vision of life as it really is, that can and does subsequently arise from time to time. In grim contrast you are also now more acutely aware than ever before of your own selfish behaviour and the inevitable suffering that comes with passionate involvement with the world. So you flip from one extreme to the other. Sometimes you experience intense longing for sensory stimulation, or extreme aversion and ill-will.

At other times you experience beautiful states of mind when you are aware of the perfect simplicity and purity of life and see magic and mystery all around you. You are able to distinguish other people's unwholesome behaviour too and find it unpalatable, directly experiencing the suffering that they cause themselves and those around them.

This perception is, of course, correct. It is also a reflection of the inner turmoil that is unfolding within you. You do not yet have the depth of understanding or equanimity to deal properly with these insights, so they simply add to your irritation and to the yawning sense of separation from the world. You may also strongly suspect that, were you to open up about what you see, others would deride you. It can be a very lonely time.

So the stream-winner fluctuates between feeling deeply connected with all of life to feeling utterly alienated and then back again. Times when greed, hatred and delusion are raging and others when life is serene, peaceful and profound. The apparent loss of the "eye of *dhamma*" is hard to bear, as is the suffering that comes with acute awareness of defiling states of mind.

It can be an intense and vulnerable time, full of painful paradox. Strong urges to seek out and reconnect with that profound serenity through the indulgence of the senses may arise. The cessation, however, of pain and restlessness fleetingly brought about through continual exploitation of such things as alcohol, drugs, sex or shopping centres will never be enough. Excess in such behaviour merely provokes intense self-disgust and reinforces a growing dissatisfaction with the world.

Occasionally a stream-winner might fall into the trap of thinking that he or she is bi-polar or even schizophrenic. It has been known for someone in this predicament, without the advantage of the council of an understanding teacher, to seek out medical advice or psychoanalysis. This is not necessary, however, and any such help will be of only limited value. In point of fact, far from being all wrong, life for a stream-winner is actually going very well and a competent teacher will be able to reassure him or her of that. Everything is most definitely as it should be.

Stream-winning is transitional, as is every other part of the path. Any spiritual training is an in-between phase of life where we learn to relinquish old habits and assumptions so that we can embrace a radically different way of seeing life. Transitions are always troublesome. In Sufism they have an expression that beautifully depicts the path as being like, "a bridge of hair over a chasm of fire."

Far from being a sickness, the trouble has been created through actually seeing life rightly. So this situation is not wrong, it is perfect and normal that we should experience such dilemmas at this time. The description offered in this chapter paints something of a worst case scenario. If someone is genuinely doing their best to live ethically and in accordance with mundane right view then this will do much to ameliorate the situation.

Solace abounds for the stream-winner. Yes, you are having trouble because you are seeing the fetters of greed and hatred right up close and it is painful. Take heart, however, as you are going to become fully enlightened and, what is more, in a strange kind of way, you know that.

The Buddha stated that should individuals do no more meditative work from this point onwards, they will be reborn no more than seven times before making a complete end of suffering. If they continue to practise they will reduce this amount greatly and can, potentially, realise *nibbāna* in this very life. Further, from this point it is impossible to fall into an unfortunate rebirth, so you are safe.

The Buddha said that this glimpse of the beyond is like seeing a well from a distance. Now you know that it is there, but it is still too far away for you to drink from its waters as you would wish. You will reach it, but first you must deal with what is in front of you. The way to deal with the fetters of greed and hatred is exactly the same as how you dealt with the preceding three. By turning the attention back to the systematic observation of the arising and passing away of things, over and over again.

Knowledge

The root cause of all psychological distress is *avijjā*, ignorance, the wilful avoidance of reality. Ignorance is perpetuated in order to maintain the assumption of our own separateness, the belief in what some people call the soul or ego. One of the ways we try to avoid existential uncertainty and prop up our view of self is through the accumulation of knowledge. Knowledge is power and power affords us a measure of control in an otherwise unpredictable world. For those engaged in the pursuit of the higher knowledge of enlightenment, this fundamental aspect of our nature needs to be fully comprehended. We risk, otherwise, falling into spiritual conceit.

To explain, here is a personal example. During my travels in India during the mid nineteen-nineties I read books by the Indian teacher Jiddu Krishnamurti. To this day I hold his words in the greatest esteem and what he wrote has undoubtedly had a major impact on my life. At the time I was also writing my own journal which I kept as part of my desperate efforts to make sense of the world. One day, however, I threw every last one of those copious volumes of frantic scribbling in the bin. Why? It was because I had a moment of stark realisation, that I was a fraud. Looking at my journal entries, I saw that all they consisted of was a sterile rehashing of Krishnamurti's words. I realised that I did not know whether what I had written was actually true or not, because it did not come from my own experience. It was all mimicry, second-hand knowledge at best and therefore it could not, in and of itself, set me free.

In hindsight I am glad that I went through that whole period. On the one hand, what was essentially memorising the words of someone I considered to be enlightened did subsequently come in very useful once I had discovered mindfulness and wise reflection. On the other hand, I also learned a very valuable lesson, that intellectual appreciation of a subject is not at all the same thing as direct understanding.

Perhaps if someone repeats publicly what he or she has read and thought about, that person may fool some of the people some of the time into believing that they are wise. Why, however, would anyone want to do that? The answer is, of course, conceit. It is to bolster the ego, the sense of "I am." It is using the spiritual life not to transcend the view of self, but as yet another way of trying to impose and reinforce the ego as an absolute reality.

I am not the only one to have gone through this kind of process. In his book *Life as a Siamese Monk*, the venerable Kapi-lavaddho Bhikkhu, who was my teacher's teacher, tells a similar story. For him, the same recognition came during a lecture he gave on Buddhism as a layman and directly led him to ordain in Thailand as a Theravada Buddhist monk.

To spout religious or spiritual ideas and doctrines to others without the real experience of them is high-minded ignorance. Just because you read about it in a book and thought about it, does not mean for one moment that you have actually realised it. Intellectual appreciation is not at all the same as wisdom.

This is also true when it comes to reading about other ways people see the world, such as the theories developed by quantum physicists; a perennial favourite amongst meditators. It is well known that descriptions of the behaviour of sub-atomic particles bear an uncanny resemblance to the ancient mystical teachings found in Hinduism, Buddhism and Taoism. For *Indra's Net* read *Zero Point Field*.

Many fascinating books have been written about the parallels between them and it is undoubtedly a tantalising subject, but ultimately how helpful is it? Science is one discipline, the spiritual path is something quite different. Although both are intent on understanding life, they are not at all the same thing as they employ radically different methodologies.

Exploring similarities between the quantum world and mystical descriptions of enlightenment might be extremely edifying and may well expand your intellectual knowledge base, but it will not increase your wisdom one jot. Science is about accumulating knowledge and power by looking at the objective world. Meditation on the other hand is about eradicating the ignorance that causes suffering by looking directly at your subjective experience. Science seeks to prove what has been assumed in the first place. Conversely, meditators are practising to free themselves from all assumptions.

Given these fundamental differences, if you commandeer scientific findings in an attempt to authenticate your spiritual beliefs in the eyes of the secular world, but without properly understanding them, beware. The proper yardstick for assessing claims in the scientific community is to provide verifiable objective evidence for your claims. If you cannot, then you are guilty of what I call high-minded ignorance and scientists know it. They call it "spiritual woo-woo."

Not even an enlightened being can prove objectively that there is a beyond of the world as normally understood, but then he or she does not have to prove it. As meditators we are under absolutely no obligation to conform to the diktats of the scientific world. They are different spheres of knowledge.

"Proof" for the meditator is the direct, intuitive experience of reality, insight-wisdom, that leads to the reduction and elimination of suffering. It is transformative in a way that science can never be. As one physicist put it, "In principle, I know that I am made of stardust but, in all honesty, it doesn't feel like it."

If scientists want to experience the reality behind what the Buddha taught then they would need to be willing to set aside their assumptions and accumulated knowledge. They would need to accept spiritual instruction, learn how to meditate, investigate their own subjective experience and see whether suffering is reduced as a consequence. For this is the appropriate yardstick in this discipline.

★ ★ ★

Reading about enlightenment and how to go about realising it is a crucial supporting condition for a meditator. The mere accumulation of knowledge, however, collecting more and better descriptions, making comparisons and drawing conclusions, will not produce enlightenment.

Imagine that you have friends who go to Tenerife on holiday and whilst there they send you a postcard. There is a beautiful photograph on the front and on the back it is written, "Having a lovely time, wish you were here." From that you think this must be what Tenerife is like. If the next year they go back and they send you another postcard, is this taking you closer to Tenerife? No, not one jot. It might give you more of an inkling as to what Tenerife might be like, but in no way is it the same as being there.

When it comes to postcards from "beyond" no matter how many you are sent, no matter how eloquent the descriptions, they can never take you there. Their role is to educate, elucidate and inspire, but that is their limit and the practicing meditator must always bear this in mind.

The accumulation of knowledge is born of the desire to avoid the suffering inherent in reality and for a meditator to seek either salvation or personal status simply through becoming knowledgeable is an anathema to the spiritual life. Anyone can read a book.

For the intellectually minded this makes meditation very difficult. Often their academic appreciation of the Buddha's teaching races far ahead of their meditative skills and this can cause a great deal of confusion, misapplication and distrust of real practice.

It is like reading a car manual from cover to cover, over and over until you feel that you have completely understood how a car works. The moment, however, you put your head under a bonnet for real, you experience the petrol fumes and the greasy muck inside which you were never prepared for by your pristine intellectual model. Disgusted, you recoil. It is the same with meditation.

The intellectual discovers the reality of his or her mind is a lot hotter, dirtier and far more unpredictable than their accumulated knowledge of the teaching had led them to believe. In fear they recoil back to the apparent safety of their accumulated knowledge.

Wisdom and intellect are not the same thing. For wisdom to flower, intellect must be put to one side. True meditation involves learning to put aside thinking because thinking is the outcome of all our accumulated knowledge and experience. Thinking reinforces the impression that life is predictable, manageable and under "your" control and therefore perpetuates illusion.

Only in the absence of thought can an unpremeditated insight into life arise. For insight-wisdom to emerge, you must first comprehend how thinking is bound up with the wilful desire to avoid looking directly at reality.

Consistently restraining from indulging thoughts further after they have arisen eventually brings mental clarity and a sense of spaciousness. It is then possible to be mindful of and investigate each new moment without any assumption or expectation about what will happen. Resting content in the moment, watching things arise and pass away, it is then possible to comprehend life in ways never known before.

Love

The Buddhist path is a training in love. It is designed to teach us what love is, not just intellectually, but really to show us what love is. By following the guidance offered, we cultivate our own capacity to love and be loved and, ultimately, we come to realise the most wonderful transcendent love. This is the love to which artists, philosophers and poets allude and for which all beings secretly long. The problem is, of course, defining exactly what we mean by this word. What is love?

Some people, when they think of love, are actually concerned with greed. They "love" the things they can acquire and consume, and from which they can derive pleasure. This includes that perennial favourite pastime of lovemaking. For many people gratification of the sexual impulse is what they consider to be love. Actually, any form of attraction whereby we appreciate the beauty or good qualities in something may be considered to be a form of love.

With regard to the Buddha's teaching, some people mistake the idea of non-attachment to mean that you cannot love anything anymore. This suggests that they very much regard an emotional dependency upon someone or something as being love. As in, "Oh Stan, promise you'll never leave me!"

Finding one's soul-mate and having an intimate bond with another human being is very much regarded in society as love. For some of us it may be an experience that is all too fleeting and seems to remain forever unrequited but, nonetheless, it is a form of love most people believe in and aspire towards.

There is also love in the sense of having a passion for something, whether it is an interest in pottery, meditation or in trying to save the world. Any form of caring, showing kindness and friendliness can be regarded as love. People who visit our Centre for the first time often comment on the simple, clean and tidy way it is kept. Impeccability is a form of love. The reason it is kept that way is because it helps to promote positive and tranquil states of mind. The love generated in maintaining a well kept environment and treating objects with care is definitely communicated to others.

Generosity is another form of love. Not just in giving material gifts, but by offering your full and undivided attention, such as perhaps when a friend is not very happy and wants to talk about a problem. Sometimes this can be a real test of one's patience and it takes a certain amount of restraint and renunciation to listen attentively and be of service to others. It is in fact an act of disinterested love, which is compassion in action.

You have, finally, the love that is opening up to the wonder and mystery of reality as it really is. This is the transcendental love that comes with the recognition of the truly infinite and unified nature of all life, and its realisation is the culmination of the spiritual search.

All these definitions of love fall into three broad categories: those that consist of entirely selfish behaviour, those that include all relatively unselfish behaviour and those that transcend notions of "selfhood" all together.

The Buddhist path teaches us how to restrain and let go of selfish preoccupations and behaviours, that "love" which exploits and hurts both us and others purely for our own gratification. It is training us in developing and making much of relatively unselfish behaviours like generosity and kindness, and all activities of a caring, friendly and compassionate nature. These bring with them a really positive self image and a lovable nature. It shows us, finally, how to realise for ourselves this transcendental love, this love that is absolutely accepting of all life just as it is.

Ironically, it is our emotional dependency upon the things of the world that is preventing us from spontaneously being in love with all of life. When we get attached to something, to anything, we immediately create division and fear, the fear of the loss of that thing. Whether we develop attachments to material things or to the things of the mind they will all inevitably let us down. Ultimately, life is uncontrollable. The fundamental nature of all things is to change and become other.

Attachment is not love. Some people get very confused about this. For example, attachment to one's children and love for one's children are two completely different attitudes. To be attached to a child means that there is an emotional dependency on that child for something. For instance, the parent might have expectations about what they want for the child. Whereas love for the child would mean teaching him or her right from wrong and trying to provide opportunities and a chance in life, but allowing the child to grow without expectation as to how he or she should turn out. Love does not have the same needy quality that attachment does. Love does not produce fear.

The absence of attachment is an entirely positive thing. You cannot know what love is while you have attachment; not really. The objective in observing the transient, ungraspable and uncontrollable nature of life, is to let go. In letting go, you stop projecting your own wants, fears, worries and neurosis onto life. Through the absence of the "warping" such attachments cause, you can finally see what is truly there.

Whilst you have attachment to things, you have a divided mind. It is not at peace, not happy. This is because it is always worried, it is always fearful about the loss of the things it depends upon. Whereas when there is no attachment, there is no worry, there is no fear and no longing for life to be one way or another. The truly happy mind, the truly peaceful mind, is an undivided mind. It is not grasping after life, so it just rests and enjoys what is there.

Whilst there is a division between "me" and "that" at work, whilst there is a sense of duality then there is a constant partitioning of life and, hence, conflict. In the absence of that false dichotomy, however, there is just love.

For anyone who has concentrated successfully, say giving their full, undivided attention to the rise and fall of the breath, there is just the most blissful peace and contentment. This is because, at that time, there is no comparing, there is no wishing life to be different, there is no dualistic-awareness at all. There is just the sheer experience and it is blissful, it is peace. Until, that is, a thought arises like, "I wish this would last forever." This comparison re-establishes the perceptions of time and space, and the idea of a separate "self" or conscious witness. At this point the peace instantly vanishes and the mind is once again divided.

Rather than seeking a temporary reprieve from that sense of division through concentration, practising *vipassanā* shows us that the presumed division between "me" and a separate universe is fundamentally false. It is a complete misperception. Understanding the false as false, you no longer take seriously the appearance of division and separateness.

When you finally see through this veil of illusion, you then realise what the mystics have been talking about all this time, and what the poets, artists and philosophers allude to but never quite seem to realise themselves. You comprehend that everything has a common, unifying quality, but one that yet defies description.

Each time you try to name it, you delineate and separate and create a new sense of division. So you are simply left with this nameless love for all things, knowing that all things are not things. They are all the same thing yet different at the same time.

You realise that love is our natural state, that love is the undivided state, and knows no opposite. You can see people with "love" tattooed on the fingers of one fist and "hate" on the other, but these are not opposites. The opposite of hate is desire, not love.

Enlightenment is very much desire-less, but it is not loveless. It is not tangled up with life, it is freedom from forever pulling and pushing, manipulating and controlling, and it is neither tolerant nor intolerant.

In our natural non-deluded state we do not take comparisons between the opposites of good and bad seriously, or right and wrong, or should and should not. You realise that life as it presents itself is perfect, just as it is, whatever appears to be there.

It is a love, not just of particular aspects of life, but of life itself. It is not even acceptance, because acceptance has the connotation of choice and therefore division. And enlightenment, call it what you will, is utterly beyond choice. It is absolute freedom of being. There are no choices to be made. It is all inclusive, wherein there is neither accepting nor rejecting. You just know that everything is inherently perfect and there is just this limitless reservoir of indefinable love.

★ ★ ★

It is a cold late autumn afternoon, the cloudless sky is deep blue and the sun hangs low over the horizon. As you enter the forest you notice that there isn't a breath of wind and the trees are silent and unmoving. A carpet of dry golden leaves greets you and you choose to walk carefully, not wishing to disturb them. As you walk deeper into the wood a hush descends and you feel the exhilaration that comes only when you commune alone with nature. A light mist hangs delicately around the trees helping to create an aura of light and peace. You stop to take it all in and notice at once that the only disturbance in the forest had been the crackle of leaves under your feet. As shafts of light arc across your path you see that dying leaves are noiselessly falling from the trees, each leaf momentarily catching the sunlight as they twirl to the ground. As they come to rest on the forest floor they make the most delicate "tiff, tiff, tiff" sound. All around, the whole three hundred and sixty degrees, everywhere the falling leaves create this marvellous, delicate symphony and you are captivated with delight at the majestic and infinite power of what is all around you. Your heart is filled with silent laughter, contentment ripples within you like a gently burbling stream and you simply stand and take in the wonder of it all. Just this is enough, it is free and it is everything. You have finally woken up and there is nothing more you need to do.

Dhamma Talks

Question: Could we talk about how trial and error are essential to the learning process?

Paul: Why is trial and error essential to the learning process?

Student 1: If you play safe all the time, you stay within the zone of what you already know, then you do not learn anything new.

Paul: You remain within the habitual culture of the mind.

Student 1: Yes, so you have to take a chance.

Paul: What is the fear? Presumably, the fear is that by stepping out of our normal way of doing things, something will happen. What might that be?

Student 1: It will hurt in some way. I will get hurt in some way.

Paul: Yes, anything else?

Student 2: You do not know what is going to happen.

Paul: Yes, the fear is that I will lose what I have got, or I will not get what I want, if I change my ways. Or I might lose control and then anything could happen. All of which implies an assumption that you know what will happen, but in reality you do not, it is the unknown. So it does all boil down to uncertainty and being prepared to go into the unknown. If we always remain within our habitual mode of doing things, then that suggests there is an emotional attachment to something, and that if you step out of your normal way of doing things you put it at risk, whatever it is.

So it is self-concern that stops somebody from trying something new. You will never get anywhere in meditation if you are not prepared to experiment, and experimentation is trial and error. But isn't that preferable? Doesn't that make the meditation something quite exciting, and something quite exploratory? A willingness to experiment brings enthusiasm to what is going on, rather than the drudgery of going through the motions in exactly the same way every time and never really applying oneself. Actually saying, "I'm going to rip it up. I know I have got habitual ways of doing things, but I am just going to rip those up. I am going to be mindful and when I come across them I am going to say, 'No, I'm not going to do it like that.'"

When you realize that you are just dabbling in some displacement activity, you need to exercise some strong intent to come out of that. Get focused, devote yourself to the task at hand and get re-energised. There needs to be an active involvement with what is going on, not just habitually doing things by rote, half-asleep. Thought needs to go into it, wise reflection and a strong determination to go at it again, and meet reality head-on. Even if that means getting it wrong or whatever it is that you fear. That is how to tackle meditation. It is this active involvement that makes it a dynamic learning process.

If someone is frightened of getting hurt by the trial and error, what sorts of things will help to cushion the blows?

Student 3: You can recollect times when you did try another approach and it had a very positive effect.

Paul: Good, a recollection of past times when you have stepped out of the norm, tried to do something a little bit differently and everything felt so much more vibrant and alive as a consequence. Perhaps your approach did not work as intended, but it really does not matter because, either way, you learned a really valuable lesson through taking a risk.

Student 3: Even if it was painful?

Paul: Well, it is going to be painful, you can guarantee, *(laughter)* because if you are learning you are bound to get things wrong, so it is going to be painful. I remember one time, I was in the garden by the eucalyptus tree feeling very despondent because the meditation was all wrong and I just could not go on proverbially "bashing my head against a brick wall." I was feeling so down and then the thought arose, "I must be doing something wrong. I must be misapplying myself in some way. It has to be, that is the only explanation." And suddenly what was closed became open and this whole new area of potential investigation emerged. What was it that I was doing? I did not know, but by being mindful of the problem I could find out. But can you see that I had first to reach that point of, "I can't go on!" before then realizing, "Oh, actually, I can." *(laughter)* But there has to be pain there, because it is the pain that forces us to reconsider.

Sorrow is your guru. If that sorrow is the pain of perpetual non-achievement of your aims in life, then at some point you have got to accept that there must be another way. If that means admitting not knowing yourself what this other way might be, then it seems sensible to let go of your pride and go and ask someone who does know. Immediately you are in a new headspace, letting go of self-concern brings you out of the old habit and open to trying something that might seem a bit different, perhaps even radical. You are tossing everything up in the air and you are looking to see how it comes back down again. At least it is going to be a new pattern, at least you are feeling dynamic, inspired, and alive again. You are back on the frontier.

Apparently researchers have found out that people are happier the more uncertain their lives are, and the more certain their lives are the unhappier they become. During the war people were said to be a lot happier because no-one had any certainty about their future. It is interesting, isn't it?

And what do we know about the enlightened being? They never know what is going to happen next. They live a life full of uncertainty and yet they are full of love for life. It all makes sense, doesn't it? The more self-concern there is, the more desire there is for solidity, certainty and permanence, which leads to dullness, apathy and risk-aversion. The less self-concern there is, the more confidence there is in life, the more willingness there is to take risks and take life as it comes. And therefore there is more dynamism, there is more awareness, more mindfulness. There is more ability to trial things, to explore and find out how things work. Embracing uncertainty and lessening self-concern are definitely the way to go.

Student 1: I was thinking you have got to give the trial a decent go, not chopping and changing all the time. But then it is difficult knowing how long to give it, and not letting it go on too long when you are just repeating errors and not learning.

Paul: Well, that is when you have got to use wise reflection, and retain a clear comprehension of your purpose, and not forget why you are trialling it. After all, you are trialling meditation and you are trialling the reclusive life. It is not set in stone, it is not forever. It is a trial to see what happens, to find out what it gives you and what it feels like, because it has got to end. It ends for everybody. The whole of life is an experiment in that sense.

Student 3: I suppose we have strong conditioning. You know, when we are young we get taught a very simplistic idea of right and wrong.

Paul: Well, some questions are rightly to be answered with a simple yes or no, but not every question. There are different kinds of question. Life questions are not that easy. Meditation questions are not that easy to answer and finding solutions often needs to be done on a trial and error basis. This is why you need clear comprehension and wise reflection, and to know that you are experimenting.

The way you overcome a doubt is by having excessive confidence. Choose one particular route and find out where it takes you. I had one of those in Sri Lanka. I was in a forest and had been given directions. There was one route that took me deeper into the forest, and another route that took me around a bend and led to what appeared to be a sheer cliff. I could not see where it was taking me beyond that, so I thought that cannot be right it looks way too dangerous. So I went down the other way, and within 100 metres or so I found the path had come to a dead end. I knew definitely that was not the right way, so I trekked back. If I had forgotten why I started going down that path I could still be there now. *(laughter)* So you have to remember it is trial and error, and then there is a natural point you reach where you are free to say, "This is not working, it is time to reconsider."

Student 3: I suppose in a sense it is not really an error. It is a result, isn't it?

Paul: Well, you have learned so much from it. I maintain that for anyone who succeeds at this practice, who has gone through the entire path and come out the other end, they bow down to all the decisions and all the mistakes they made in their life. All the terrible things they did and all the terrible things that were done to them; the embarrassments, the heartbreaks and whatever else. They turn round and they bow down in genuine gratitude because they would not have accomplished what they accomplished, not just in terms of the path itself but everything that led to them even approaching the path, without all of that. Sorrow is your guru. It really is, because it forces you to reconsider. It forces you, in the end, to practise some wise reflection and to try something else. Come out of the dull ritual of habit, be brave and throw all the cards up in the air to see where they land.

Question: Why is it that observed feelings change from unpleasant to pleasant to neutral over a period of observation of the same sense-door contact?

Paul: Can you ever observe the same sense-door contact twice?

Student 1: No, not ultimately.

Paul: And we are talking ultimately here. Notice how our assumptions trip us up. Often, in the early days, meditators will believe that it is the same sense-door contact occurring again and again, and the same feelings repeating. But is that the case?

Student 1: It is not really true.

Paul: It is not true at all. Can you see how this question is formulated from a wrong premise? You can never experience the same sense-door contact. It is always a new experience. Therefore the feeling that arises due to that new contact, could that ever be the same feeling?

Student 1: Not exactly...

Paul: Can I give you an illustration of what I mean here? You are aware of how washing powder advertisements claim that their product is "new and improved." Is that logically consistent? *(laughter)* If something is new can it also be improved?

Student 1: Compared with the old one?

Paul: Well, if there was an old one and this is a new one, is it improved?

Student 1: No.

Paul: It is either new or it is improved, it cannot be both. So, to get back to the point, a new contact arises, a feeling arises conditioned by that contact. Is it the same feeling?

Student 1: No.

Paul: It is not at all, is it? It is a completely new feeling. Are we all agreed on that? *(laughter)* Okay, so we can rephrase the question: I have noticed that, with each subsequent sense-door contact in a series, it is possible for different kinds of feeling to arise. How does this happen?

Student 1: I saw it happening, but it was confusing. Why does that happen?

Paul: Let me give you a scenario. You are meditating in the Shrine Room, and someone starts using a pneumatic drill outside. Sound arises and a feeling arises conditioned by that sound. Of the three basic kinds of feeling, pleasant, unpleasant and neutral, which would you expect to arise first? If you are looking at it really closely, what would you say?

Student 1: Unpleasant.

Student 2: I would say neutral. But then it would also depend on the volume of the pneumatic drill, if it was a shock... but I would still say neutral actually.

Paul: We are looking right at the very first instance here, the initial arising of that sound before any perceptions occur.

Student 3: I am torn between pleasant...

Paul: Pleasant!?

Student 3: ...and neutral.

Paul: Okay, but not unpleasant? Personally, from experience, I would say neutral. Subsequently, perceptions arise such as: pneumatic drill, worker, outside, noisy or disturbance and the like. These are all perceptions that are not related to our idea of what should happen in our meditation. A comparison is made, it is believed that something alien has invaded the meditation. Okay, what happens next in terms of mental processing?

Student 2: There is a resistance to it.

Paul: There is resistance to it. Resistance is *kamma*, craving for life to be different, it is action. What are the results of action?

Student 2: You get feelings and perceptions coming up.

Paul: As the sound of the drill continues, what will the feeling component be as a resultant of that prior resistance?

Student 1: It is unpleasant.

Paul: Okay, so you have now got an unpleasant feeling arising on a sense-door contact, but it is not the same sense door contact, it is a new sense-door contact. Mental contacts in the form of perceptions then arise that reinforce the resistance, producing yet more unpleasant mental feeling. Now let's imagine this is an experienced meditator. They recognise what is going on, what do they need to do here? They have unpleasant mental feelings and life is not as it should be. What do they do, what is the next step?

Student 2: Restrain the resistance

Paul: Restrain the resistance because you cannot do anything about the noise. Unless you get out of your chair, go out into the road and say, "Excuse me I'm meditating. Do you mind not doing this right now?" *(laughter)* It is not going to happen is it? You have got to stay with it, you cannot move. So the only alternative is to restrain the craving for life to be different at that time. What might you do instead of resisting? What might you choose to do?

Student 2: Investigate, because it is actually a big object.

Paul: Yes. If you look meditatively at the sound of a pneumatic drill, you can begin to detect discreet sounds within the sounds and you start to see that all those sounds arise only to pass away again. The sensory contacts still occur, but if you chose to investigate your immediate experience in terms of transience what feeling might arise?

Student 2: You might well get pleasurable interest arising from the investigation as you become fascinated with what is going on.

Paul: You might listen to those sense-door contacts and start by experiencing painful or neutral feeling. That investigation itself might then provoke pleasant feeling to arise from the pleasurable interest. Do you see what I am getting at? You have this whole series of sense-door contacts and dependent upon your response to those contacts you get different kind of feelings arising. If you resist they will be unpleasant, if you get interested and observe them they can be pleasant.

But all those contacts, the feelings and the responses to them are marked by the sign of transience and that is the important thing to remember. It is never the same contact, the same feeling, the same response. Life is always new, it is never old. In that way even the most supposedly un-meditative environment can become a meditative one.

But to answer your question, that is how it is that observed feelings can change from unpleasant to pleasant to neutral.

Student 1: Can I ask, with regard to aversion, at what point in the cycle would you label it as a hindrance?

Paul: I cannot answer that question because it is almost like asking how long a piece of string is. If you keep on developing mindfulness you will begin to detect the pattern more and more quickly. If you are lost in aversion then there is no mindfulness present at that time. Where there is craving, there is always ignoring.

But for every meditator there exists a window of opportunity to become mindful of what is going on. It takes a fair amount of wise reflection. Perhaps at the end of that hour's meditation you come out thinking, "Well I never got going with that. What happened there?" If there is a willingness to reflect, you start to recognise patterns, "Oh hang on there was an aversion to the sounds coming from outside."

So next time it might actually start to become evident within the meditation itself that something is not right. So some wise reflection goes in right there, "Hang on a minute, what is going on? What is it that I am resisting here?" The painful feelings, the resistance, the restlessness, the sense that something is amiss, are all calls to be mindful, to observe closely what is going on.

With increased mindfulness and reflection, recognition of the pattern comes closer and closer to the actual event itself. Eventually a point is reached where mindfulness becomes so strong that you are able to observe that process unfold in real time. So it is a gradual unfolding over time, from confusion as to what is going on, to just being right there with it.

Ultimately what we are talking about is a choice-less awareness of the process taking place, for it is through understanding the process that you are free of it.

Student 1: What about the situation where a meditator is forcing it, trying to get in early to make sure the hindrances cannot take over?

Paul: I would suggest relaxing. Adopt an attitude of allowing whatever wants to enter the mind to enter, but remaining mindful and self possessed. Be interested to find out what does happen and allow the meditation to take care of itself. This means accepting the possibility for the mind to get lost, to get distracted, or to become confused. I know that sounds paradoxical, but it is only because hindrances are allowed the space to come up in the first place, that it is possible to be mindful of them.

In order to be aware of what they actually are and to label them clearly, you have to risk losing your mindfulness, your clarity, or anything you wanted the meditation to be. Yes, you might get swept away by hindrances from time to time, but does that situation last? We all get lost in thinking from time to time. However, through that lack of self-concern, through that lack of resisting and manipulating and trying to control, you can actually see much more clearly what is going on. You realise that you have a much wider playing field than you thought. You thought you had to keep mental activity tightly bound, but you do not.

As long as mindfulness is there, along with enthusiasm and interest in investigating and reflecting, then you can actually relax and you discover that meditation is a far more enjoyable experience for it.

Question: What changes after enlightenment?

Paul: So what does change after enlightenment?

Student 1: Nothing and everything.

Paul: Indeed, but only an enlightened mind really understands what that means.

Student 1: Yes.

Paul: Here is a metaphor. Imagine you have come up against this huge, impenetrable wall. It goes out infinitely in both directions and you cannot find your way around, over, under or through it at all. Eventually a door materializes so you go through, but when you turn round and look at the wall from the other side, you find that there never was a wall there at all. I love that. *(laughter)*

We say "everything and nothing" because it is not so much the discovery of something new, but rather it is ceasing to ignore the way things have always been. Nothing is gained as such, but what is lost is delusion. Can you see how complete that is? It is not an improvement of your situation. It is not a relative improvement of your lot. It is an absolute transformation. It is an absolute one-hundred percent transformation. So, it is the same universe and yet completely different, because it is fundamentally different to the way you formerly understood it to be. Yet, the universe in and of itself has not changed.

I could describe a walk in the countryside with all the sensory impressions and mental activities involved. Everyone can relate to that, everyone understands exactly what that is. But the one thing you cannot adequately express is the one thing which makes the difference, which is the total comprehension that there is no duality. That does not mean there is no intelligent, conscious experiencing. There is, but conscious experience is a concatenation of an infinite number of transient impersonal conditional forces of mind and matter at play with one another. Meaning that there is no need for an abiding core to the experience or an entity behind it all, pulling the strings. There is no duality. There is just that. There is just the manifestation of the universe, conscious experience arising and passing away. Entirely intelligent, happy, peaceful, joyful even, and completely unfathomable. It always retains that sense of utter mystery.

In a more poetic mood we might say that it is pure love. But it is not the cloying, clawing kind of love that wants anything. It is totally disinterested love. It is just the love of the moment, arising in the moment with whatever that moment brings. This is a huge change from before enlightenment when there is all the self-concern and so forth, which can never be love. Although one is entirely vulnerable, of course, at all times, it is a total ending of all self-concern. There is no sense in which, even in a dangerous situation, there is any danger to "me." Yet there is the total comprehension that one must be careful.

What changes after enlightenment? You finally realize why there is no point in giving descriptions. They are all false. Whatever you say it is, that's what it's not. *(laughter)* I think the best use for descriptions is making known that enlightenment is real, and that its discovery is the only worthwhile thing to do with this short life. It is telling you that anything else that might appear to be worthwhile is actually illusory, a cul-de-sac, and is just keeping you asleep and unaware of the real goal of human life. And it is telling you that once you get there you will never regret it. You will never regret all the hard work it took to finally understand. No matter what your starting position was or what state your spiritual faculties were in to begin with. It is the answer. Big capital letters! It is the answer and yet no answer at all.

So what changes at enlightenment? As you quite rightly state, everything and nothing.

Student 1: The question came about because, in a recent Q&A, you gave us the idea of someone with absolutely no involvement or interest in the spiritual search and who has never heard of enlightenment. And then imagining that person walking into a room where there was an enlightened teacher sitting there with an unenlightened student who is asking the teacher about enlightenment, wanting to know what it is. You said that the person walking in does not perceive any qualitative difference between the teacher and student in this regard, he just sees two people sitting there. You said that the teacher sees no difference between any of them either and then you asked what the distinction was between the outlooks of the teacher and the newcomer.

Paul: Yes.

Student 1: It cannot be seen on the outside, certainly.

Paul: The person that walks in the room has no comprehension that there is any difference, because they have no comprehension that enlightenment exists. They are blinded by ignorance. The enlightened mind has realized non-duality, and does not take seriously false dichotomies such as I am enlightened and you are not. It only seems to bother the person who is under training. Given that the enlightened being knows that there is no difference between enlightened and unenlightened, doesn't that give pause for thought about the state of mind of the trainee who is still concerned about the difference? The student is still dividing life up in that way, because she still wants to achieve enlightenment. There is still an attachment to it and that is the last thing to be renounced prior to the true realization. The student may well think, "If there is no difference, in that case I am already enlightened." Then, paradoxically, the enlightened teacher will say, "You have no right to say that, because you are most definitely not."

My idea in saying all this is not to clarify things for you. The idea is to bamboozle you completely. *(laughter)* It is to encourage you to stop speculating about what it might be, and just work diligently at developing mindfulness so that you can find out for yourself.

Specifically, that kind of imagery is offered to the person who has completed the entire *vipassanā* training, because the only thing they are still worried about at that point is whether they are enlightened or not. And they have got a justifiable claim to worry about that, because they have perfected their view and they are still wondering, "Well, am I enlightened or not?" Really, even a description of a walk in the woods is intended for someone at that point, because they will be pondering, "Yes, but that is what happens when I experience that," and then asking themselves, "Well, what's the difference?" So it is actually very useful to ask the question and it is useless all at the same time. *(laughter)* When someone finally realizes that it is pointless to ask the question, because it will never be answered, they let go. Then at some point after that they realize that they do know, they do understand, but in a way that they just could not possibly have manufactured themselves. It comes to you. All you can do, finally, is to abandon even the attempt to become enlightened.

But you cannot abandon the attempt to become enlightened until your view is perfected, because you are still bound up with fetters. You are still bound up with defiling states and you have to be free of all attachment before enlightenment can come and visit.

Appendices

Appendix I

Condition–Dependent Origination – *paṭicca-samuppāda*

This is the Buddha's account of the causal structure of the round of existences. It explains the conditions that sustain the cycle of birth and death and make it revolve from one life to another.

Dependent on ignorance arise *kamma* formations.
Dependent on *kamma* formations arises consciousness.
Dependent on consciousness arises mind and matter.
Dependent on mind and matter arise the six sense bases.
Dependent on the six sense bases arises contact.
Dependent on contact arises feeling.
Dependent on feeling arises craving.
Dependent on craving arises clinging.
Dependent on clinging arises becoming.
Dependent on becoming arises birth.
Dependent on birth arise decay-and-death, sorrow, lamentation, pain, grief and despair.

Thus arises this whole mass of suffering.

Blinded by ignorance of the true nature of reality and driven by craving, an individual engages in wholesome and unwholesome actions (*kamma* formations). To consciously experience the pleasant and painful results of all such action necessitates the production of mind and matter, and the six sense bases. Still deep in ignorance, upon contact with these resultants, the individual is overwhelmed by the craving to enjoy more pleasant experiences. He clings to those he already has and tries to avoid painful ones, thus generating the inevitability of future resultants. In this way the cycle spins relentlessly until the ignorance at its core is removed by insight-wisdom.

1. Ignorance 2. Formations	Past active phase; equivalent to 8-10
3. Consciousness 4. Mind and matter 5. Six sense bases 6. Contact 7. Feeling	Present resultant phase; equivalent to 11-12
8. Craving 9. Clinging 10. Becoming	Present active phase; equivalent to 1-2
11. Birth 12. Decay and death	Future resultant phase; equivalent to 3-7

The same fundamental pattern is operative at all levels of conscious experience, from moment to moment, within an individual life and from life to life.

Appendix II

The Five Aggregates – *pañcakkhandhā*

Materiality
Feeling
Perception
Mental Formations
Consciousness

The practice of *vipassanā* is the observation of the constituents of ultimate reality as they arise in our moment to moment subjective experience. This is in order to comprehend directly their true characteristics as being transient, unsatisfactory and non-self. To facilitate this analysis, the Buddha organised all such phenomena into distinct groups or heaps, known as the five aggregates.

Although not exhaustive, the lists included here give further details of what each aggregate consists.

1) Materiality

The Four Great Elements:
1. Extension
2. Temperature
3. Motion
4. Cohesion

Sense Faculties:
1. Eye
2. Ear
3. Nose
4. Tongue
5. Body

Sense Objects:
1. Visible form (shape and colour)
2. Sound
3. Smell
4. Taste
5. Tactile object (= extension, temperature, motion)

Sexual Phenomena:
1. Femininity
2. Masculinity

Communicating Phenomena:
1. Bodily intimation
2. Vocal intimation

Other Material Phenomena
Life faculty
Nutriment
Space element

2) Feeling

> *Three-fold division*:
> 1. Pleasant
> 2. Unpleasant (painful)
> 3. Neutral (neither pleasant nor painful)
>
> *Five-fold division*:
> 1. Pleasant bodily
> 2. Unpleasant bodily
> 3. Pleasant mental
> 4. Unpleasant mental
> 5. Neutral
>
> *Six-fold division:*
> Feeling arising from sense-contact via...
> 1...eye
> 2...ear
> 3...nose
> 4...tongue
> 5...body
> 6...mind

3) Perception

> *Six-fold division*:
> Perception arising from sense-contact via...
> 1...eye
> 2...ear
> 3...nose
> 4...tongue
> 5...body
> 6...mind

4) Mental Formations

Universals (common to all types of consciousness):
  Contact
  Volition
  One-pointedness
  Mental life-faculty
  Attention

Occasionals (found in most but not all types of consciousness):
  Initial application
  Sustained application
  Decision
  Energy
  Pleasurable interest
  Desire-to-do

Unwholesome:
  Delusion   Envy
  Restlessness   Avarice
  Greed   Wrong view
  Hatred   Shamelessness
  Sloth   Fearlessness of wrong-doing
  Doubt   Conceit

Wholesome:
  Faith   Non-greed (renunciation)
  Mindfulness   Non-hatred (loving-kindness)
  Fear of shame   Compassion
  Fear of blame   Appreciative joy
  Equanimity   Lightness of mind
  Tranquillity   Non-delusion (wisdom)

5) Consciousness

Seven-fold division:
1. Eye-consciousness or seeing
2. Ear-consciousness or hearing
3. Nose-consciousness or smelling
4. Tongue-consciousness or tasting
5. Body-consciousness or touching
6. Mind-consciousness
7. Mind-consciousness-element★

★takes any of the preceding six types of consciousness as object

Glossary of Pali Terms

A note on Pronunciation

The pronunciation of Pali words is fairly straightforward. There are only a few points to remember:

c – "h" as in "church"
ñ – sounds like a Spanish "ny" as in "señor"
ṃ (with dot underneath) – a nasalised sound like "ng" as in "sing"
ā – as in "far"
ī – as in "meet"
v – pronounced as a "w" in some Theravada Buddhist countries such as Thailand

There are a couple of other sounds indicated by a dot under a t or over an n, but the untrained western ear generally cannot distinguish the differences between these and the sounds produced from letters without dots below or above.

avijjā – ignorance, blindness, unawareness of the true nature of reality i.e. ignorance of the Four Noble Truths and Condition Dependent Origination etc. It also includes ignoring i.e. the wilful turning away from reality. It is the fundamental condition upon which all craving and subsequent suffering arises.

Bodhisatta – a being who aspires to become a future Buddha and whose life is dedicated to that end. When talking about his life before his realisation, Gotama always used this epithet.

Brahma-cariya – pure or holy life. It is a term for the life of a Buddhist monk or nun, or anyone who is training, in earnest, to realise enlightenment.

Buddha – the awakened one. It is specifically the being who rediscovers and proclaims the lost path to enlightenment. Along with the *Dhamma* and the *Saṅgha*, it forms the Triple Jewel to which Buddhist practitioners traditionally go for refuge. The recollections of *Buddha*, *Dhamma* and *Saṅgha* are also formal meditations.

Buddha-dhamma – the teachings of the Buddha.

Dhamma – This is a word with a variety of meanings and different usages including law, doctrine, the constitution or nature of a thing, and ultimate phenomenon.

dukkha – pain, both physical and mental. It is an umbrella term for all forms of suffering including disease, old age, death, grief, sorrow, lamentation and despair, as well as the fundamentally unsatisfactory nature of all conditioned phenomenon on account of their impermanence.

kamma – wholesome and unwholesome volitional actions of body, speech and mind i.e. all action performed under the delusion of selfhood.

kamma-vipāka – the results of past volitional action that are experienced as the pleasant and unpleasant feelings and perceptions that arise upon sense-contact. Also includes the initial arising of subsequent volitional tendencies.

mettā – the wholesome mental quality of friendliness. It is also the name given to the formal meditation practice of loving-kindness.

nibbāna – the non-conceptual realisation of the way life really is, non-duality, the cessation of suffering. It is the universal goal of freedom and happiness to which all beings aspire. It can be regarded as the absence of the three unwholesome roots of craving, hatred and delusion.

Pali Canon – the earliest extant collection of discourses that comprise the whole of the Buddha's original teaching. They have been preserved in the ancient language of *Pali* and handed down through countless generations by the Theravada Buddhist monastic tradition.

paññā – wisdom, insight, investigation. It is the mental quality of non-delusion, the penetration of the appearances of things and clear comprehension of the laws and processes of life as they really are i.e. the Four Noble Truths etc. Wisdom is one of the three Buddhist trainings, along with ethics and mental control.

pāramī – perfections. These are ten qualities to be developed in the course of the training that are necessary supports for the realisation of enlightenment. They are: generosity, ethics, renunciation, wisdom, energy, patience, truthfulness, determination, loving-kindness and equanimity. Their development strengthens compassion and reduces selfish preoccupation.

samādhi – concentration, fixing the mind on a single object. As one of the three trainings, along with ethics and wisdom, it can be thought of in a more general way as mental control.

saṃsāra – perpetual wandering. It is the relentless cyclical process of birth and death, driven by ignorance and craving, of which this single lifetime represents only a tiny and fleeting fraction.

Saṅgha – is the name for the community of monks and nuns, and in a wider sense, also includes lay students and supporters. The term too is used to signify all those men and women who are either enlightened or are destined to be so. Along with the *Buddha* and *Dhamma*, it forms the Triple Jewel to which Buddhist practitioners traditionally go for refuge. Recollection of the *Saṅgha* is a formal meditation practice.

sīla – discipline or ethical conduct, specifically with regard to speech, bodily action and means of livelihood. It is one of the three trainings, along with mental control and wisdom.

vipassanā – meditation practice that generates insight-wisdom into the transient, unsatisfactory and selfless nature of existence, destroying the roots of greed, hatred and delusion and all possible clinging attachment to the world.

These books are available by mail-order via our website:

Postcards from Beyond	£12.95
The Purpose of Life	£8.95
A Meditation Retreat	£6.95
Modern Buddhism	£6.95
The Unfolding of Wisdom	
softback	£7.95
hardback	£9.95
Inner Tranquillity	£7.95
Buddhism: The Plain Facts	£5.95
Buddhist Character Analysis	£5.95
Buddhism in a Foreign Land	£7.50
Life as a Siamese Monk	£7.95

All profits from the sale of this book go directly to the Aukana Trust, a registered charity (No 326938) dedicated to the promotion of the Buddha's teaching.

Under the spiritual guidance of **Paul Harris**, the Aukana Trust provides a wide range of facilities from introductory evening classes in meditation and Buddhist philosophy right through to full-time monastic training. All the activities are held at the House of Inner Tranquillity in Bradford on Avon.

If you would like further information, please contact:

Aukana Trust
9 Masons Lane
Bradford on Avon
Wiltshire
BA15 1QN
England

e-mail: info@aukana.org.uk
web: aukana.org.uk
Telephone: (01225) 866821
International: +44 1225 866821